McCALL'S
Introduction to
MEXICAN
COOKING

McCALL'S
Introduction to
MEXICAN
COOKING

Edited by Linda Wolfe

GALAHAD BOOKS · NEW YORK CITY

Copyright © 1960, 1961, 1962, 1963, 1964, 1965, 1966, 1967, 1968, 1969, 1970, 1971 by
The McCall Publishing Company. All rights reserved. No part of this work may be repro-
duced or transmitted in any form or by any means, electronic or mechanical, including
photocopy, recording, or any information storage and retrieval system, without permission
in writing from the publisher.

Library of Congress Catalog Card Number: 73-92825
ISBN 0-88365-200-5

Published by arrangement with Saturday Review Press,
division of E. P. Dutton & Co., Inc.

Printed in the United States of America

Contents

Illustrations follow pages 24 and 40

McCALL'S
Introduction to
MEXICAN
COOKING

Introduction

Mexican cuisine is not only colorful and tangy, but immensely varied. Yet for some strange reason many Americans seem to think of it as a bowl of chili con carne (not really Mexican at all) and one big tortilla. Nothing could be further from the truth, as this book will show you. Mexican cooking mingles an ancient and developed Indian culinary tradition, that of the Aztecs, with one of Europe's finest cuisines, that of Spain.

The Aztecs, when Cortés first encountered and conquered them, were a singularly advanced people. They had an elaborate system of writing, built magnificent pyramids and temples, and placed great emphasis upon dining. One of the soldiers who came to Mexico with Cortés later wrote a memoir of his adventures. In it, he described witnessing the meals that were served to Montezuma:

His cooks had upwards of thirty different ways of dressing meats and had earthenware vessels so contrived as to keep them always hot. For the table of Montezuma, himself, above three hundred dishes were dressed; and for his guards, above a thousand. . . . They daily cooked fowls, turkeys, pheasants, native partridges, quail, tame and wild ducks, venison, wild boar, reed birds, pigeons, hares and rabbits and many other things.

As the memoirs of the Spanish soldier reveal, Montezuma was a veritable gourmet. Bathed by beautiful girls before he dined, he then ate in private surrounded by screens. His food was kept hot with a device similar to today's candle warmer; a small pool of oil was kept burning in a pan beneath each serving dish. When the emperor had eaten his hot meal, he would relax and digest his food while watching jesters and buffoons. It was no wonder that so sophisticated a people as the Aztecs knew and cleverly used many foods, nor that they were able to entice the appetites of the Spaniards with these foods, even though all of them were previously unknown in Europe.

Perhaps the single most important food the Spaniards tasted in Mexico was the tomato. It is today impossible to imagine Spanish cuisine without the tomato—nor for that matter, Italian, nor our own. The little red fruit was highly prized by the Indians, who called it *tomatl.* They carved and copied its shape onto many stones and pieces of pottery, and they mixed it in many different sauces. The conquistadors brought tomatoes back home with them, but when the first Europeans tasted the raw red fruit they expected it to be sweet and were disappointed by its tartness. Then a chef at the Spanish court, familiar with the stories of the elaborate sauces made by the Aztecs, decided to cook some tomatoes in olive oil and onions, thus creating the first tomato sauce as we now know it.

Turkeys, too, were first introduced to the rest of the world from Mexico. The conquistadors loved the flavor of this new bird, and found room for turkey chicks and breeding hens among their sacks of gold on their ship. They also brought with them sweet potatoes, corn, avocados, eggplants, beans, sweet and spicy peppers, vanilla, chocolate, and a host of other new foods, most of which went on to become integral to Spanish cuisine.

The Spanish, on their part, introduced to them cattle, pigs, sheep, and the notion of cooking with animal fat, frying in lard, a technique that is basic to today's cooking in Mexico. Out of the culinary interbreeding of the two peoples emerged the fanciful Mexican cuisine.

Mexicans love to eat; those who can afford to manage to eat four meals a day. Breakfast starts the day. In the cities, this tends to be light, consisting of sweet rolls and coffee or hot chocolate, but in the country, breakfast may be very large, the rolls and hot drinks being accompanied by eggs and even steak. At midday, most Mexicans have their main meal, or *comida,* which frequently consists of as many as seven courses. This meal, a two-hour affair, is the center of daily life for Mexicans. For it, the husband comes home from work; the children, from school. After the meal, there is usually a siesta, a virtual necessity after so many courses. *Comida* begins with an appetizer, followed by soup. After the soup comes a course called dry soup, which is not really soup at all but a starchy dish, either cut-up tortillas or noodles or rice, which has been cooked in a broth or sauce and is moist. Next there may be a fish course, and after that, the main course of poultry or meat, accompanied by salad and vegetables. Then there is a sweet, and at last the meal ends with tea or coffee.

Later, at around six in the afternoon, it is time for *merienda,* a small meal similar to the English teatime. Tea is not drunk at *merienda,* however. Instead the Mexicans drink New World drinks, coffee or the hot chocolate that was beloved by Montezuma. And with it, they eat cakes and cookies and pastries. Then, sometime between eight and ten in the evening, there is supper. For those who have made the *comida* their big meal, supper, or *cena,* will be light. But some Mexicans have adopted the American custom of eating lightly at noon and having their main meal at night. Thus more and more restaurants in Mexico serve big late-night meals.

The presentation of food is quite important. The Mexicans are the most fanciful craftsmen in the world. Their brightly colored pottery plates decorated with birds and animals, their intricate silver dishes from Taxco, their exquisite tablecloths from Oaxaca, their woven mats and their hand-blown glasses and even their great primitive earthenware jugs and casseroles are all a delight to the eye. The presence of such articles on a Mexican table makes the entire meal immediately inviting and exciting.

Mexican pottery and tablecloths and glassware are available throughout this country, usually at reasonable prices; it is a good idea to use some of these accessories if you are planning a Mexican dinner or party. The colorful nature of these objects will say to your guests not only, "See what an imaginative table I've contrived," but, "The meal that follows will be just as imaginative and gay."

Mexican drinks, such as tequila and the wine punch sangría, have become immensely and justifiably popular in the United States in the last few years, and should certainly be included in your planning if you intend to serve drinks. Tequila is made from the sap in the starchy roots of the agave plant, a succulent which also provides fiber for twine, mats, and clothing. It is normally colorless, although some types of tequila are aged in a way that gives them a pale yellow color. While it has a reputation for being very potent, it is actually no stronger than whiskey. It can be drunk straight or made into a delicious cocktail called a Margarita, in which lime juice, sugar, and a dash of Cointreau or triple sec are added to the tequila. Because tequila and salt go together beautifully (Mexicans often drink their straight tequila by putting a pinch of salt on the back of one hand, tossing the salt into their mouth, then downing the tequila with the other hand), Margaritas are served in cold glasses that have been dipped into coarse salt so that the salt forms a crystal frosting around the glass edge.

Sangría is a cool delicious wine drink that originated in Spain but is now drunk throughout Latin America and Mexico. It can be a very alcoholic drink if you include brandy and Cointreau in the punch, as some people do, or just a mildly alcoholic fruit juice and wine combination. To make the former, mix a bottle of Spanish wine (one pint, seven ounces) with two tablespoons of sugar, a sliced lemon, and a half of a sliced orange. Stir until the sugar dissolves, then add two ounces of Cointreau, two ounces of Spanish brandy, and twelve ounces of club soda. Pour this over a tray or two of ice cubes into a handsome pitcher, and let the punch cool for fifteen to twenty minutes. It will make a refreshing drink for four. If you prefer the less heady version, you may mix the wine with lime or orange juice instead of additional alcohol. Here is a way to make a mild sangría that will provide sixteen 6-ounce servings: Combine a quart of dry red wine with two reconstituted cans of frozen limeade and a large bottle (twenty-eight ounces) of club soda. Pour it over ice cubes into a pretty pitcher and garnish with orange slices.

What should you serve to eat at your Mexican dinner or party?

Mexican cuisine begins now, as it did in the time of the Aztecs, with tortillas. When the Spanish first came to Mexico, they observed the Indian women grinding corn meal by hand and then cooking little pancakes on dry griddles. The Spanish—as has everyone who has since tasted them— came to love the little pancakes. They are not difficult to make (see pp. 62–63). In Mexico and some parts of the United States, a specially ground corn meal called *masa* is available. Or you can make tortillas with ordinary corn meal. Or you can buy tortillas ready-made. They should be present at any Mexican meal, served warm, stacked within a warm white linen cloth, and then placed in a colorful straw basket. They accompany all Mexican foods and form the basis of some of the more famous Mexican dishes, such as enchiladas, tostadas, and tacos.

A tostada is a toasted tortilla topped with cheese, chopped meat, hashed beans, shredded lettuce, and tomatoes. Tacos are tortillas which are wrapped around some meat, chicken, or other filling, and they are usually fried. Enchiladas are tortillas which are rolled around a filling, which again might be meat or chicken or cheese or sausage, and then baked in a sauce or fried and dipped in sauce. Once you have made your basic tortillas, you will find many recipes that call for them in the chapter on main dishes. Beef enchiladas, chicken enchiladas with red chili, chili and tortilla pie, beef tacos with green chili sauce, are just a few of the unusual dishes you can make with tortillas.

Tamales, another famous Mexican specialty, are also made with corn meal dough, but the method of preparation is very different from that used to make tacos or enchiladas. To make a tamale, the corn meal dough is spread on a cornhusk, a filling is placed on top, the husk is rolled and tied, and the little package is steamed. Tamales with pork is a typical Mexican dish. Slightly more unusual is the tamale pie.

Tamales and tortillas are cooked in a thousand different ways in Mexico, depending upon the imagination of the cook. Indeed, a whole range of dishes based on them is called *antojitos,* or whimsies, in Mexico. An *antojo* is a spur-of-the-moment urge. Once you have learned a few basic varieties, you will be able to create your own, easily, satisfying whatever culinary whimsy you have.

Most *antojitos* are made from corn, in itself another important Mexican food. Corn was unknown in Europe until the Spaniards encountered it on the Caribbean islands and in Mexico. The Mexican Indians lived a more civilized and agricultural life than did those of the islands, and their corn grew in carefully tended fields. It had been known to the Indians for many hundreds of years. Recent archeological research has unearthed the ancestor of corn in Indian caves throughout the New World, a strange plant with ears only about one inch long. From this midget the Mexican Indians had developed many improved varieties of corn by the time of the Conquest, some adapted to the cool highlands, others to the tropical lowlands. From the corn plant the Indians made pancakes, the ancestor of today's tortillas, grinding the grain in stone mortars and baking the pancakes on a stone griddle. Often they would eat as many as twenty at a meal, and sometimes they used the little flat cakes as plates, receptacles for sauces heaped upon them—the original version of today's tacos and enchiladas.

So essential was corn to the Indians that they virtually deified it. They had a legend, similar to our Prometheus legend, in which the god Quezacoatl took pity on man for his weak and hungry condition and stole for him seeds of the corn plant, the food of the gods, so he might raise it and grow strong. Some Indians believed that corn was the basic substance from which the gods had made mankind, the very "flesh of man."

But corn alone doesn't make for a very balanced diet. Curiously it was as if the primitive Indians knew this. Alongside their corn they invariably grew beans, a food much richer in protein. Sometimes the climbing beans were planted so close to the corn that they could use the corn stalks as natural poles. Today, perhaps the most popular vegetable dish throughout Mexico is refried beans in which cooked kidney beans are fried, then mashed and flavored with tingling spices.

Another food that is typically Mexican and which is served in many intriguing ways in Mexico is the avocado. While avocados tend to be expensive in some parts of the United States, they grow so profusely in tropical climates that even poor Mexican families can enjoy this delicious fruit frequently. The most popular way of preparing avocado is to mash the insides with tomatoes and onions and spices, making the famous guacamole. It too is an ancient Indian dish, a Mayan specialty.

No account of Mexican cuisine would be complete without mentioning chilies. All peppers are called chilies in Mexico, whether they are sweet and green or red and fiery hot. There are over ninety different varieties of chilies in Mexico, and a pepper afficionado can easily distinguish the different flavor of each. To most Americans a chili pepper is a hot pepper, and all such peppers seem to taste alike. Nevertheless, chilies are quite popular here, though usually a mild variety is preferred. Or, Americans find the use of a prepared chili powder satisfactory for conveying the taste of chilies and for avoiding the nuisance of dealing with them. Because they contain an oil in their flesh and seeds that can irritate the skin and eyes, it is advisable to wear rubber gloves when peeling chili peppers and to wash the hands thoroughly afterwards. Mexicans usually toast their chili peppers first, then peel them, remove the seeds and membranes, and soak them in milk or water until they are soft enough for cooking. Since chili powder is readily available and easy to use, the recipes in this book rely on this prepared seasoning rather than the fresh ingredient to give this very special Mexican flavor.

Chilies are the basis of most Mexican sauces, and Mexico is a country of sauces. In a Mexican marketplace, one can purchase some tortillas, then wander for an hour from stall to stall, sampling from the earthenware bowls of different sauces, and never encounter two exactly alike. The ancient Maya called all sauces moles, but today *mole* refers to one special Mexican sauce, the most exquisite of all, which is traditionally served over turkey. There is a beautiful legend connected with this sauce. It recounts the woes of some sixteenth-century nuns in the remote convent of Santa Rosa. Their archbishop decided to pay them a visit, but failed to notify them until shortly before his arrival. Like any woman who has faced a culinary emergency when her husband calls at five in the afternoon to say he is bringing the boss or the new client home for dinner, the nuns of Santa Rosa were distraught because none of their food seemed fine enough for such a distinguished visitor. Being closer to God than some of us, they began to pray for guidance, and as the story goes, it was granted them. They were inspired with the idea for a new dish. They roasted a turkey, and while it was cooking, they began to cut up and grind every ingredient they had in the convent kitchen. Into the grinding bowl went tomatoes, onions, almonds, bananas, garlic, tortillas, sugar, raisins, and innumerable other things. The final inspiration was to grind in a little chocolate. They cooked this sauce and poured it over the roasted turkey. All who tasted it pronounced the sauce godlike in its flavor.

Today the kitchen at Santa Rosa is a national museum. And every Mexican woman is proud of her mole. The nuns' original recipe was extremely complicated; the one we offer in this book is a somewhat simpler version, but one that will produce the same divine results.

The chocolate that the nuns added to their sauce at the last moment was itself a product of Mexico. It was the Spaniards with Cortés who were the first Europeans to taste chocolate. They observed that Montezuma drank a dark, sweet drink with his meals, sometimes made cold with pieces of snow from the white-capped mountains. The Indians called it *xoxo-atl*, which the Spaniards translated as *chocolate*. The Indians were very pleased to share their knowledge of this drink, but they found it difficult to describe to the conquistadors the little wild orchid pod, *thilxochitl*, with which they flavored the drink. The Spaniards named it *vainilla*, or little pod, and debated which flavoring they preferred, chocolate or vanilla, as has the rest of the world ever since.

As befits the people who gave chocolate and vanilla to others, Mexicans love sweets and have invented many different kinds. But curiously their favorite dessert is a Spanish one, a caramelized custard called flan. Flan and many other dishes that are traditionally Spanish, such as paella, chick-pea soup, and gazpacho, are found in Mexico's cuisine today, broadening and enriching it.

The American cook will find that cooking in the Mexican style will give her a repertoire of recipes that are more flavorful than many of our own, as exotic as the dishes of the Orient, and as time-honored as the dishes of Europe. Of the hundreds of recipes that comprise Mexican cuisine, those presented here are in themselves enough to start the American cook on a voyage of discovery and conquest as exciting as that of Cortés.

Appetizers & Soups

Whimsical food, tidbits to tickle and excite the palate, is a Mexican specialty. But it is sometimes difficult to decide when such a tidbit is an appetizer and when, served in quantity, it is suitable for a main dish. The appetizers in this chapter are all excellently suited for a first course at dinner or for a cocktail party. Particularly delicious are the turnovers, called *empanadas* in Mexico, little crisp dough envelopes filled with tasty mixtures of meat or fish or cheese.

A number of recipes that are included in other sections of this book may also be served as appetizers, such as guacamole or tacos. When it comes to Mexican appetizers, or to first-course food in general, it is wise to familiarize yourself with all the dishes that comprise a cuisine, then select your own starter to go with whatever else you are planning to serve. Just remember that the appetizer should reflect the cook's own whimsy, her own favorite way of exciting the interest of her guests in what is to follow.

Mexican soups are substantial and filling. Some of the famous soups of the country are inheritances from Spain; others are Mexico's own. In Mexico, it is customary to make soup very slowly in an earthenware pot; the thick porous sides help to retain the flavor of each of the many ingredients no matter how long the soup simmers. We have adapted the Mexican style to suit our own more hurried north-of-the-border pace, but the results of these recipes provide the same tropical flavors and warmth.

APPETIZERS

Beef Empanadas

Filling
2 tablespoons butter
½ cup chopped onion
¾ pound ground beef
2 large ripe tomatoes,
   chopped (1 pound)
1 can (4-ounce size)
   green chilies, drained
   and chopped
1 teaspoon salt

1 bay leaf

Pastry
1½ cups unsifted
   all-purpose flour
¾ teaspoon salt
½ cup shortening
4 to 4½ tablespoons ice water

Salad oil for deep-frying

1. Make filling: In hot butter in large skillet, sauté until tender. Add eef, and sauté until no longer red.
2. Add tomatoes, chilies, salt, and the bay leaf. Simmer, stirring occa-onally, 30 to 35 minutes, or until most of liquid has evaporated. Remove om heat; discard bay leaf.
3. Meanwhile, make pastry: In medium bowl, combine flour and salt. 'ith pastry blender, cut in shortening until well blended. Sprinkle with e water; stir with fork until mixture holds together. Shape into a ball.
4. Divide pastry into 18 pieces. On lightly floured surface, roll each ece onto a 4-inch round. Place about 2 tablespoons filling on one half of ch round; fold over other half. Press edges together with fingers, to seal; ess edges with tines of fork.
5. In electric skillet or deep saucepan, slowly heat salad oil (1½ to 2 ches deep) to 375°F. on deep-frying thermometer.
6. Gently drop beef pies, a few at a time, into hot oil. Cook, turning ith slotted utensil, until golden brown on both sides—3 to 4 minutes.
7. Drain on paper towels. Serve hot.
Makes 1½ dozen.

Shrimp Empanadas

Filling
2 large very ripe tomatoes
   (1 pound)
½ pound shrimp, shelled
   and deveined

3 tablespoons olive oil
½ cup chopped onion
1 small bay leaf
1 teaspoon salt
¼ teaspoon pepper

Dash sugar
1 tablespoon cornstarch
¼ cup cold water

Pastry
1 cup water
1 tablespoon butter

½ teaspoon salt
1 cup sifted all-
   purpose flour
1 egg, slightly beaten
1 cup bread crumbs

Salad oil for deep-frying

1. Make filling: Peel tomatoes, and press through sieve to remove seeds and make a purée. Cut shrimp into small pieces.

2. In hot oil in medium saucepan, sauté onion with bay leaf, salt, and pepper until golden brown—about 3 minutes. Add puréed tomato and the sugar; bring to boiling. Reduce heat, and simmer, stirring occasionally, 35 minutes. Add shrimp, and simmer 10 minutes longer.

3. Mix cornstarch with cold water. Stir into shrimp mixture. Bring to boiling, stirring constantly; boil 1 minute. Remove from heat; discard bay leaf.

4. Meanwhile, make pastry: In medium saucepan, heat 1 cup water, the butter, and salt to boiling.

5. Stir in flour briskly; heat, stirring, until mixture forms a ball and leaves side of pan. Remove from heat; let stand 15 to 20 minutes, or until cool enough to handle.

6. Turn out onto lightly floured board; knead for 3 minutes. Then roll to 1/16-inch thickness. Cut with 3½-inch round cookie cutter. Place about 1 teaspoon filling on one half of each pastry round; fold over other half. Press edges together with fork to seal.

7. Brush filled pastry, top and bottom, with beaten egg; then dip in bread crumbs. Place on waxed-paper-lined tray. Refrigerate, covered, several hours, or until ready to cook.

8. To cook: In electric skillet or deep-fat fryer, slowly heat salad oil (from 1½ to 2 inches deep) to 375°F. on deep-frying thermometer.

9. Gently drop shrimp pies, a few at a time, into hot salad oil. Cook, turning as needed with slotted utensil, until golden brown on both sides—about 5 minutes.

10. Drain on paper towels. Serve hot.
Makes about 20.

Salmon-Stuffed Avocados

1 package (8-ounce size)
   cream cheese, softened

2 cans (7½-ounce size)
   salmon, drained

2 teaspoons Worcestershire sauce	3 avocados, black or green skinned
1½ teaspoons salt	1 tablespoon lemon juice
⅛ teaspoon pepper	

1. In large bowl, with wooden spoon, beat the cream cheese with salmon, Worcestershire, salt, and pepper until fluffy.

2. Halve avocados lengthwise; remove pits. Brush cut sides with lemon juice to prevent discoloration.

3. Fill hollow of each half with cream-cheese mixture. Refrigerate until well chilled—about 1 hour.

Makes 6 servings.

Sardine Appetizers

2 cans (3¾-ounce size) skinless and boneless sardines, packed in oil	1 can (4-ounce size) pimientos, drained and diced
	¼ cup olive oil
1 medium onion, peeled and finely chopped	Toast strips or unsalted crackers

1. Preheat oven to 350°F.

2. Carefully lift sardines out of can, and arrange, spoke fashion, in 9-inch pie plate.

3. Arrange onion and pimientos, in alternate rows, between sardines.

4. Pour olive oil over all. Bake uncovered, 30 minutes. Cool; then refrigerate until cold.

5. Serve with toast strips or unsalted crackers.

Makes 12 hors d'oeuvre.

Crisp Relishes with Avocado Dip

1 ripe avocado	1 bunch radishes
1 small cucumber	8 pitted green olives
1 envelope onion-dip mix	¼ cup mayonnaise
6 small carrots	Tabasco
1 bunch celery	

1. Peel avocado; remove pit. Mash with fork in medium bowl. Stir in ¼ cup mayonnaise, the onion-dip mix, and 4 drops Tabasco; mix well. Chill, covered, in freezer until serving—15 minutes.

2. Pare cucumber; wash and pare carrots; cut cucumber and carrots

lengthwise into sticks. Wash radishes; trim. Wash celery; trim leaves. Remove inner stalks. Chill all in bowl of ice and water.

3. Drain vegetables from ice water, and dry on paper towels. Arrange on platter with avocado dip.

Makes 5 to 6 servings.

Piña Acapulco

1 pineapple	Olives
3 to 4 sausages cut up	Radishes

1. Split the pineapple lengthwise.
2. Spear it with bite-sized sausages, olives, radishes, etc.

Makes 6 to 12 servings.

Tostadas

Shortening for frying	1 cup grated sharp Cheddar cheese
10 frozen tortillas	

1. Heat about ¾-inch shortening in medium skillet. Fry tortillas, one at a time, about 1 minute on each side.
2. Drain and cool on cake racks lined with paper towels.
3. Sprinkle tortillas with cheese. Place under broiler 5 to 6 inches from heat; broil about 1 minute, or until cheese is melted and bubbly.

Makes 10 servings.

Chili con Queso

2 tablespoons butter	¼ teaspoon salt
¼ cup finely chopped onion	½ pound Monterey Jack
1 can (8¼-ounce size)	cheese, cubed (sharp
tomatoes, undrained	Cheddar may be substituted)
1 can (4-ounce size)	¼ cup heavy cream
green chilies, drained	
and chopped	Tostaditas

1. In hot butter in medium skillet, sauté onion until tender. Add tomatoes, chilies, and salt, mashing tomatoes with fork. Simmer, stirring occasionally, 15 minutes.

2. Add cheese cubes, stirring until cheese is melted. Stir in cream. Cook, stirring constantly, 2 minutes.

3. Remove from heat, and let stand 15 minutes. Serve warm, as a dip with tostaditas (canned tortillas, cut in wedges and fried until crisp) or, if desired, with corn chips.

Makes 6 servings.

SOUPS

Cream-of-Chicken Soup

2 egg yolks	¼ teaspoon pepper
1 can (12¾-ounce size) chicken consomme, undiluted	3 tablespoons dry sherry
1¼ cups heavy cream	1 tablespoon coarsely chopped watercress
1 teaspoon salt	

1. In top of double boiler, combine egg yolks and consomme; mix well.

2. Cook, over hot water and stirring constantly, until mixture thickens and forms coating on metal spoon—8 to 10 minutes.

3. Remove from heat. Stir in cream, salt, and pepper.

4. Cook, over hot water and stirring occasionally, about 5 minutes, or until very hot. Stir in sherry.

5. Serve at once. Garnish each serving with watercress.

Makes 4 servings.

Chick-Pea Soup with Sausage

1 pound dried chick peas	2 cans (13¾-ounce size) chicken broth
2 tablespoons olive oil	
1 cup sliced onion	1 bay leaf
1 clove garlic, split	4 cups water
½ pound boiled or cooked ham, diced	1 cup sliced, pared carrots
½ pound link pork sausage, diced	2 cans (8-ounce size) tomato sauce

1. Pick over chick peas, discarding any imperfect ones. Place in bowl; cover with water; let stand overnight.

2. Next day, rinse peas with fresh water; drain. Set aside.

3. In hot oil in a 6-quart kettle, sauté onion, garlic, ham, and sausage until onion is tender but not browned—about 15 minutes.

4. Add peas, chicken broth, bay leaf, and 4 cups water; bring to boiling. Lower heat, and simmer, covered, 2 hours.

5. Stir in carrots and tomato sauce; simmer, covered, 2 hours longer, or until peas are tender.

Makes 8 to 10 servings.

Gazpacho

2 large tomatoes, peeled (1¾ pounds)	⅓ cup red-wine vinegar
1 large cucumber, pared	¼ teaspoon Tabasco
1 medium onion	1½ teaspoons salt
1 medium green pepper	⅛ teaspoon coarsely ground black pepper
1 pimiento, drained	2 cloves garlic, split
2 cans (12-ounce size) tomato juice	½ cup croutons
⅓ cup olive oil	¼ cup chopped chives

1. In electric blender, combine 1 tomato, ½ cucumber, ½ onion, ¼ green pepper, pimiento, and ½ cup tomato juice. Blend, covered, at high speed, 30 seconds, to purée the vegetables.

2. In a large bowl, mix puréed vegetables with the remaining tomato juice, ¼ cup olive oil, vinegar, Tabasco, salt, and pepper.

3. Refrigerate mixture, covered, until well chilled—2 hours. Refrigerate 6 serving bowls.

4. Meanwhile, rub inside of skillet with garlic; reserve garlic. Add rest of oil; heat. Sauté the croutons until they are browned; set aside.

5. Chop separately remaining tomato, cucumber, onion, and pepper. Place in separate bowls, along with separate bowls of croutons and chopped chives. Serve as accompaniments.

6. Just before serving time, crush the reserved garlic; then add to the chilled soup, mixing well. Serve in chilled bowls.

Makes 6 servings.

Fish Soup

Broth	1 small carrot, pared and finely diced
2 tablespoons olive oil	
2 tablespoons butter	1 stalk celery, finely chopped
1 small onion, finely chopped	(½ cup)

1 sprig parsley, finely chopped	**Seafood**
1 clove garlic, crushed	1 (½ pound) lobster tail,
3 vegetable-bouillon cubes	cooked and shelled
1½ quarts water	½ pound raw shrimp,
1 can (8-ounce size)	shelled and deveined
tomato sauce	½ pound red snapper, boned
1 cup white wine	¼ pound sole fillet
½ cup dry sherry	1 pint shucked clams
¼ cup cognac	2 tablespoons olive oil
1 teaspoon salt	2 hard-cooked eggs, chopped
1 bay leaf	
Pinch of saffron	Slivers of French bread,
	lightly toasted

1. Make broth: In hot oil and butter in Dutch oven, sauté onion, carrot, celery, parsley, and garlic until carrot is tender but not brown—about 10 minutes.

2. Add bouillon cubes, water, tomato sauce, wine, sherry, cognac, salt, bay leaf, and saffron; bring to boiling, stirring frequently. Reduce heat and simmer, uncovered, ½ hour.

3. Meanwhile, prepare seafood: Slice lobster meat and shrimp. Cut red snapper and sole in small cubes. Cut clams in half.

4. Heat oil in large skillet. Add seafood and sauté, stirring, until heated through and coated with oil. Remove from heat and set aside until soup is ready. Then add to broth and simmer, covered, about 5 minutes, or until all fish is cooked. Garnish with chopped egg and French bread slivers.

Makes 6 to 8 servings.

Soup Mexicana

2 packages (2¼-ounce size)	½ teaspoon dried
dried tomato-soup mix	oregano leaves
2 teaspoons instant	¼ teaspoon chili powder
minced onion	6 cups water

1. Combine all ingredients in 2-quart saucepan; stir until well mixed. Over high heat, bring to boiling, uncovered, stirring occasionally.

2. Reduce heat; simmer 15 minutes, stirring occasionally. Serve at once, in mugs.

Makes 6 servings.

Albondigas Soup

Broth
½ cup finely chopped onion
1 clove garlic, minced
2 tablespoons salad oil
1 can (8-ounce size)
  tomato sauce
3 quarts boiling water
8 beef-bouillon cubes

Meatballs
¾ pound ground chuck
¾ pound ground pork
⅓ cup raw regular rice
2 teaspoons salt
¼ teaspoon pepper
1 egg, slightly beaten
1 tablespoon finely chopped
  mint leaves

1. In large saucepan, sauté onion and garlic in hot oil until golden. Add remaining broth ingredients; heat to boiling.

2. In medium bowl, combine meatball ingredients. Shape into 1-inch balls, and drop into boiling broth. Cover; reduce heat, and simmer 30 minutes.

Makes 6 to 8 servings.

Salads & Vegetables

Mexicans rely heavily on their own delicious native vegetables and fruits. Avocados are used in infinite ways, as are corn, beans, and peppers, all gifts of the New World to the Old. The Mexican attitude toward vegetables is one that Americans would do well to adopt. Recent studies have shown that many Americans avoid vegetables; as a result we may be deficient in the vitamins and minerals that vegetables provide. This is probably because we think of vegetables as a food that must be eaten plain and therefore find them bland and uninteresting. Mexicans, however, rarely eat a vegetable without first dressing it up. Their famous refried beans are mixed with onions and green peppers, corn is made into a festive pudding, and peppers are stuffed with meat or cheese to make chilies rellenos or roasted with wine and herbs to make savory sweet peppers.

Displaying the same skills that have made their weaving, pottery, silverwork, and even papier mâché among the world's most admired handicrafts, Mexicans bring a particularly artistic eye to the color and arrangement of vegetables. Mexican salads and vegetables look as good as they taste.

SALADS

Avocado-and-Red-Onion Salad Bowl

2 heads Boston lettuce, washed and chilled
1 ripe avocado

1 large red onion
4 ounces oil-and-vinegar dressing

1. Break lettuce into bite-sized pieces into salad bowl.
2. Peel avocado, and cut in large sizes into salad bowl.
3. Peel and thinly slice onion, and add to salad bowl.
4. Toss together with oil and vinegar dressing just before serving.
Makes 6 servings.

Guacamole

1 medium tomato, peeled	1 teaspoon salt
2 ripe avocados	⅛ teaspoon pepper
(about 2 pounds)	
3 tablespoons finely	Cauliflowerets
chopped green chili	Celery sticks
peppers	Carrot sticks
½ cup finely chopped onion	
1½ tablespoons lemon	
(or lime) juice	

1. In medium bowl, crush tomato with potato masher.
2. Halve avocados crosswise; discard pits; peel avocados. Slice avocados into crushed tomato. Crush with tomato until well blended.
3. Add chili peppers, onion, vinegar, salt, and pepper. Mix well.
4. Refrigerate, covered with plastic wrap, until well chilled—at least 1 hour.
5. Meanwhile, prepare cauliflowerets, celery, and carrot sticks. Refrigerate in bowl of salted water until well chilled.
6. Serve guacamole surrounded with drained vegetables.
Makes 8 servings.

Guacamole–Tomato Salad

6 medium tomatoes, skinned	2 teaspoons lemon juice
2 teaspoons salt	2 very ripe medium
1 medium onion,	avocados
finely chopped	6 lettuce leaves
1 or 2 green chilies,	3 strips crisp-cooked
finely chopped	bacon, crumbled

1. Core tomatoes; scoop out centers, and chop finely. Sprinkle inside of tomato cups with ½ teaspoon salt, and turn upside down on paper towels to drain. Chill.
2. To chopped tomatoes, add onion, green chili to taste, lemon juice, and remaining salt. Chill.

3. Just before serving, halve avocados crosswise; discard pits; peel and ash avocados (they will turn dark if allowed to stand). Blend in tomato ixture. Arrange tomato cups on lettuce leaves. Fill with guacamole; top ith crumbled bacon.

Makes 6 servings.

Guacamole Mold

2 medium-sized, ripe tomatoes, peeled	⅛ teaspoon pepper
	1 teaspoon chili powder
2 ripe avocados (about 2 pounds)	1 cup dairy sour cream
	1 cup mayonnaise
2 tablespoons lemon juice	3 envelopes unflavored gelatin
¼ cup chopped green pepper	1 cup cold water
½ cup finely chopped onion	
1 teaspoon seasoned salt	Parsley sprigs

1. In large bowl, crush tomatoes with potato masher.

2. Halve avocados crosswise; discard pits; peel avocados. Slice into tomatoes. Crush to blend well.

3. Add lemon juice, green pepper, onion, seasoned salt, pepper, chili owder, sour cream, and mayonnaise. Mix to blend well.

4. Meanwhile, sprinkle gelatin over cold water in small saucepan; let and 5 minutes to soften.

5. Place saucepan over low heat, stirring until gelatin is dissolved. Reigerate until consistency of unbeaten egg white—about 15 minutes.

6. Stir gelatin into avocado mixture to combine well.

7. Turn into a 1½-quart melon mold which has been rinsed in cold ater. Refrigerate until firm—6 hours, or overnight.

8. To unmold: Run a small spatula around edge of mold. Invert over latter; shake gently to release. If necessary, place a hot, wet dishcloth ver bottom of mold; shake again to release.

9. Garnish with parsley.

Makes 6 to 8 servings.

Tomato Salad Mold with Sliced Avocados

3 envelopes unflavored gelatin	1 can (1-pint-2-ounce size) tomato juice

⅓ cup red-wine vinegar
1 teaspoon salt
Tabasco
2 medium tomatoes,
    peeled and diced (1¼ cups)
1 large cucumber, pared
    and diced (1½ cups)
1 medium green pepper,
    diced, (¾ cup)

¼ cup finely chopped
    red onion
1 tablespoon chopped chives
3 large ripe avocados
    (about 2¼ pounds)
Lemon juice
⅓ cup oil-and-vinegar dressing

Watercress

1. In medium saucepan, sprinkle gelatin over ¾ cup tomato juice to soften. Place over low heat, stirring constantly, until gelatin is dissolved Remove from heat.

2. Stir in remaining tomato juice, the vinegar, salt, and few drop Tabasco. Set in bowl of ice, stirring occasionally, until mixture is consistency of unbeaten egg white—about 15 minutes.

3. Fold in tomatoes, cucumber, green pepper, onion, and chives unti well combined. Pour into 1½-quart mold that has been rinsed in cold water.

4. Refrigerate until firm—at least 6 hours.

5. To unmold: Run a small spatula around edge of mold. Invert over serving platter; place a hot, damp dishcloth over inverted mold, and shake gently to release. Refrigerate.

6. Just before serving, halve the avocados, remove pits, peel, and slice Brush with lemon juice. Arrange the avocado slices around the molded salad, and pour dressing over them. Garnish with watercress.

Makes 6 servings.

Olive-and-Green-Bean Salad Bowl

2 packages (9-ounce size)
    frozen, cut green beans
1 cup herb-flavored
    salad dressing
2 ounces blue cheese,
    crumbled

1 cup sliced, pitted
    ripe olives
½ cup thinly sliced
    red-onion rings

1. Cook green beans as package label directs; drain, and cool.

2. In jar with tight-fitting lid, combine salad dressing with cheese shake well to combine.

3. In salad bowl, toss green beans, olives, and onion rings. Add dress

ing; toss lightly. Refrigerate, covered, stirring occasionally, until very well chilled—at least 3 hours.

Makes 6 servings.

Cauliflower Salad

2 cups raw cauliflower broken into florets	**Dressing**
	4½ tablespoons salad oil
½ cup chopped, pitted ripe olives	1½ tablespoons lemon juice
	1½ tablespoons wine vinegar
⅓ cup finely chopped green pepper	1 teaspoon salt
	¼ teaspoon sugar
¼ cup chopped pimiento	Dash pepper
3 tablespoons chopped onion	

1. In medium bowl, combine cauliflower, olives, green pepper, pimiento, and onion.

2. Make dressing: In small bowl, combine salad oil, lemon juice, vinegar, salt, sugar, and pepper; beat with rotary beater until well blended. Pour over cauliflower mixture.

3. Refrigerate, covered, until well chilled—at least 1 hour.

4. To serve: Spoon salad into bowl, or, if desired, arrange on lettuce on individual salad plates.

Makes 4 servings.

Garbanzo Salad

1 can (14-ounce size) garbanzos, drained	4 ounces pimientos, chopped
	3 green onions, chopped
2 tablespoons olive oil	1 teaspoon salt
¼ cup wine vinegar	Dash pepper
¼ cup chopped parsley	

1. Drain garbanzos in sieve; then wash with cold water.

2. In medium bowl, combine garbanzos with remaining ingredients. Cover, and refrigerate for 2 to 3 hours.

Makes 4 servings.

Orange-and-Onion Salad

4 small oranges	2 tablespoons red- wine vinegar
1 small onion, peeled	
¼ cup olive oil	2 tablespoons water

1 clove garlic, split
¼ teaspoon salt
Dash freshly ground
   black pepper

1 quart crisp salad greens
½ cup sliced,
   pitted green olives
   (optional)

1. Peel oranges; remove white membrane. With sharp knife, cut oranges and onion in thin slices. Place in shallow dish.

2. In measuring cup, combine olive oil with vinegar, water, garlic, salt, and pepper; stir well with fork. Pour over oranges and onion.

3. Refrigerate, covered, until well chilled—at least 2 hours. Remove garlic.

4. To serve: Place greens and olives in salad bowl. Add oranges and onions (separated into rings), with the dressing, and toss well.

Makes 6 servings.

VEGETABLES

Refried Beans I

1 pound dried
   pinto beans
6 cups cold water
6 slices bacon
¼ cup finely chopped onion

¼ cup finely chopped
   green pepper
1 clove garlic, crushed
2 teaspoons salt
1 teaspoon chili powder

1. Wash beans. Turn into large bowl; cover with cold water. Refrigerate, covered, overnight.

2. Turn beans and liquid into a large saucepan. Bring to boiling; reduce heat and simmer, covered, about 1½ hours, or until tender. Drain beans, reserving liquid. Add water to liquid, if necessary, to make 1 cup.

3. In large skillet, sauté bacon until crisp. Drain on paper towels, and crumble.

4. In bacon drippings in skillet, sauté onion, green pepper, and garlic until tender—about 5 minutes.

5. With wooden spoon, stir in beans, bacon, salt, and chili powder. Cook over medium heat, stirring in reserved bean liquid a little at a time and mashing beans until mixture is creamy.

6. Turn into serving dish. If desired, sprinkle with chopped green pepper, crisp bacon bits, or strips of cheese.

Makes 6 to 8 servings.

Refried Beans II

6 tablespoons butter	1 teaspoon salt
2 cans (1-pound size) red kidney beans, drained	⅛ teaspoon chili powder
	⅛ teaspoon ground cumin

1. Melt butter in large, heavy skillet.
2. Add beans; mash well, with potato masher.
3. Stir in seasonings; cook over low heat, stirring often, until thick and bubbling.
Makes 6 servings.

Green Beans with Mushrooms

2 packages (10-ounce size) frozen French-style green beans	1 tablespoon finely chopped parsley
2 tablespoons finely chopped onion	½ teaspoon salt
2 tablespoons olive oil	¼ teaspoon pepper
3 pimientos, cut in strips	1 can (4-ounce size) sliced mushrooms, with liquid

1. Cook beans according to label instructions; drain.
2. In large skillet, sauté onion in hot oil until limp.
3. Add beans and remaining ingredients; heat thoroughly.
Makes 6 servings.

Corn and Olive Casserole

2 cans (17-ounce size) cream-style corn	1 teaspoon salt
1 package (8-ounce size) sharp Cheddar cheese, diced	⅛ teaspoon pepper
¼ cup diced green pepper	2 eggs, slightly beaten
¾ cup sliced, pitted ripe olives	1 tablespoon snipped chives
	1 medium tomato, peeled and sliced

1. Preheat oven to 350°F.
2. In a 2-quart casserole, combine corn with rest of ingredients, except tomato.
3. Bake, uncovered, 45 minutes. Place tomato slices around edge of casserole; bake 30 minutes longer.
Makes 6 to 8 servings.

Green Corn Tamales with Spanish Sauce

⅔ cup yellow corn meal	1 teaspoon salt
1½ cups water	4 sweet green chilies or
1 cup fresh raw	2 medium green peppers
corn kernels	4 pieces Monterey Jack or
1 egg	sharp Cheddar cheese
2 tablespoons salad oil	16 cornhusks, washed

1. In medium saucepan, stir corn meal into water. Cook, stirring, over low heat, until very thick. Add corn, egg, oil, and salt; stir vigorously. Cool.

2. Split the green chilies and remove ribs and seeds. (If using green peppers, cut in half, remove ribs and seeds; then parboil 8 to 10 minutes.) Insert a 3-by-½-by-½-inch piece of cheese in each chili half.

3. For each tamale, arrange 4 cornhusks, overlapping, on work surface.

4. On each casing, place large spoonful of cornmeal mixture; hollow slightly with back of spoon. Place a stuffed chili into each hollow; top with remaining cornmeal mixture. Wrap cornhusks around filling and tie ends securely with string.

5. Place on rack in large kettle over boiling water. Cover and steam 40 minutes. Serve with Spanish sauce.

Makes 4 servings.

Spanish Sauce

1 cup finely chopped	½ teaspoon salt
green pepper	½ teaspoon dried
½ cup finely chopped onion	oregano leaves
2½ cups finely	¼ teaspoon freshly
chopped tomatoes	ground pepper

1. Combine all ingredients in medium saucepan.

2. Cook over low heat, stirring occasionally, 20 minutes.

Makes 4 cups.

Fiesta Corn Pudding

¼ cup butter	½ cup coarsely chopped
1½ cups freshly grated	green pepper
corn or 2 cans (8-ounce size)	½ cup coarsely chopped
whole kernel corn, drained	sweet red pepper

½ cup coarsely chopped onion
¼ cup unsifted all-purpose flour
1 teaspoon salt
¼ teaspoon pepper

2 cups milk
1 cup (¼ pound) grated
  sharp Cheddar cheese
3 eggs, slightly beaten

1. In hot butter in large skillet, sauté corn, peppers, and onion, stirring, 2 minutes.

2. Reduce heat; cook, covered, 10 minutes, or until vegetables are tender.

3. Meanwhile, preheat oven to 350°F. Lightly grease a 1½-quart casserole.

4. Remove skillet from heat; stir in flour, salt, and pepper to combine well. Gradually stir in milk.

5. Bring to boiling, stirring. Reduce heat. Add cheese; cook, stirring, until cheese is melted and sauce is slightly thickened. Remove from heat.

6. Stir a little of cheese sauce into eggs; then pour back into rest of cheese sauce, mixing well.

7. Turn into prepared casserole. Set casserole in pan containing 1 inch hot water; bake 50 minutes, or until sharp knife inserted near center comes out clean. Serve hot.

Makes 8 servings.

Charcoaled Roast Corn

Corn, as many ears
  as desired
Butter, 2 tablespoons
  for each ear of corn

Lettuce leaves, 1 for
  each ear of corn

1. Husk corn; remove silk.

2. For each ear, cut an 18-by-15-inch rectangle of heavy-duty foil.

3. Brush each ear with 2 tablespoons soft butter. Wrap each ear of corn in a wet lettuce leaf.

4. Place each ear on foil rectangle; wrap tightly, and twist foil at ends, to seal.

5. Adjust grill 5 inches above prepared coals. Place corn at edge of grill. Grill, turning occasionally, 20 to 30 minutes, or until the corn is tender.

Chilies Rellenos

¼ pound Monterey Jack
  or sharp Cheddar cheese,
  cut into strips
2 cans (4-ounce size)
  green chilies, drained
3 eggs, separated
3 tablespoons flour

Salad oil for deep-frying
Flour

Sauce
1 can (1-pound size)
  stewed tomatoes
2 tablespoons finely
  chopped onion
1 chicken-bouillon cube
½ teaspoon salt
¼ teaspoon dried
  oregano leaves
Dash pepper

¼ cup grated sharp
  Cheddar cheese

1. Insert a strip of cheese into each chili.

2. In medium bowl, beat egg whites until they form soft peaks. In small bowl, beat egg yolks slightly. Gently fold into egg whites. Add 3 tablespoons flour, and fold just until blended.

3. In electric skillet or heavy saucepan, slowly heat 1½ to 2 inches oil to 400°F. on deep-frying thermometer.

4. Roll the cheese-stuffed chilies in flour. With large, slotted spoon, dip chilies in batter, coating generously. Gently place in hot oil, 2 at a time, and fry until golden on both sides—3 to 4 minutes.

5. Preheat oven to 350°F.

6. In medium saucepan, combine tomatoes, onion, bouillon cube, salt, oregano, and pepper; simmer, stirring sauce occasionally, 10 minutes.

7. Place chilies in shallow baking dish. Spoon sauce over top. Sprinkle with Cheddar cheese.

8. Bake, uncovered, 20 minutes, or until heated through and cheese is melted.

Makes 6 servings.

Savory Sweet Peppers

3 red peppers
  (about 1 pound)
3 green peppers
  (about 1 pound)
2 tablespoons olive oil

1 tablespoon wine vinegar
½ teaspoon salt
½ teaspoon dried oregano leaves
⅛ teaspoon pepper

1. Wash peppers; cut each in half lengthwise; remove ribs and seeds. Cut each half in fourths lengthwise.

2. Heat oil in large skillet. Add peppers and cook over medium heat, stirring occasionally, about 15 minutes, or until peppers are just tender.

3. Gently stir in vinegar, salt, oregano, and pepper.

Makes 8 to 10 servings.

Roasted Peppers

8 medium sweet red peppers (about 2½ pounds)	¼ cup lemon juice
	2 teaspoons salt
1 cup olive oil	1 small clove garlic

1. Preheat oven to 450°F.

2. Wash and drain peppers well.

3. Place peppers on baking sheet; bake, turning every 5 minutes with tongs, about 20 minutes, or until skin of peppers becomes blistered and charred.

4. Place hot peppers in large kettle; cover; let stand 15 minutes.

5. Peel off the charred skin with a sharp knife. Cut each pepper into fourths.

6. Remove ribs and seeds; cut out any dark spots.

7. In large bowl, combine olive oil, lemon juice, salt, and garlic. Add pepper quarters and toss lightly to coat.

8. Pack mixture into 1-quart jar; cap. Refrigerate several hours or overnight. Serve as an appetizer or in a tossed salad.

Makes 1 quart.

Skillet Potatoes

½ cup butter	3 pounds medium potatoes, peeled and thinly sliced (about 8 cups)
6 medium onions, peeled and sliced (about 3 cups)	
	2 teaspoons salt
	½ teaspoon pepper

1. Melt 2 tablespoons butter in large skillet; sauté onion until tender—about 5 minutes. Remove from skillet.

2. Add 3 tablespoons butter to skillet and heat. Add half the potato and sauté, stirring occasionally, until nicely browned—about 10 minutes. Remove from pan. Repeat with remaining butter and potato.

3. Layer potato and onion in skillet, sprinkling with salt and pepper. Cook over low heat, covered, about 15 minutes, or until potato is tender.

Makes 8 to 10 servings.

Mexican Rice

3 tablespoons olive oil	2 cups water
2 cups raw long-grain white rice	1 can (8-ounce size) tomato sauce
1 cup chopped onion	½ teaspoon salt
1 clove garlic, crushed	⅛ teaspoon pepper
2 cans (10½-ounce size) condensed chicken broth	Parsley sprigs

1. Preheat oven to 350°F.

2. Heat 2 tablespoons oil in large skillet. Add rice and cook over medium heat, stirring frequently, until golden brown. Turn into a 2½-quart casserole.

3. In remaining oil in same skillet, sauté onion and garlic until tender—about 5 minutes. Stir in chicken broth, water, tomato sauce, salt, and pepper; bring to boiling. Stir into rice.

4. Bake, covered, 40 to 45 minutes, or until tender. Garnish with parsley sprigs, if desired.

Makes 6 to 8 servings.

Eggs & Seafood

he excellent Mexican egg dishes derive from the days when much of he country was given over to ranching and big hearty breakfasts were he rule. Eggs ranchero, for which we give two recipes, made with cheese, omatoes, and vegetables, make a satisfying dish for any meal. On the anch they were often served with steak, as our second recipe indicates.

The equally excellent fish dishes are, for the most part, special to the oastal regions of Mexico. For many years, because of hot climate and adequate refrigeration, only the coastal people of Mexico were able to xperiment with fish. Most people think of Mexico as mountainous and nd to forget that the country possesses a long and intricate coastline mmed with palms, and with many varieties of colorful tropical fish in s warm waters. A number of Mexican fish dishes combine fish with gredients special to Mexico, as in fish in orange juice or fish with avocado uce. Fish and shellfish are also added to paella, a dish inherited from pain and cherished throughout Mexico.

EGGS

Puffy Spanish Omelet

Sauce
2 tablespoons butter
1 clove garlic, crushed
¼ cup chopped onion

⅓ cup thinly sliced celery
½ cup chopped
  green pepper
½ teaspoon salt

⅛ teaspoon pepper
¼ teaspoon paprika
¼ teaspoon dried oregano leaves
1 can (8-ounce size)
  tomato sauce
1 can (3-ounce size)
  sliced mushrooms
9 pitted jumbo ripe olives,
  thickly sliced
1⅓ cups coarsely
  chopped fresh tomatoes

Parsley sprigs

Omelet
6 egg whites
⅛ teaspoon cream of tartar
6 egg yolks
¾ teaspoon salt
Dash pepper
6 tablespoons milk
2 tablespoons butter
2 teaspoons salad oil

1. In large bowl of electric mixer, let egg whites warm to room temperature—about 1 hour.

2. Preheat oven to 350°F.

3. Meanwhile, make sauce: In hot butter in medium skillet, sauté the garlic, onion, celery, and green pepper until they are tender—about 5 minutes.

4. Add salt, pepper, paprika, oregano, and tomato sauce; bring to boiling. Reduce heat; simmer, uncovered, 10 minutes. Remove from heat and let stand until step 14.

5. Now make omelet: With mixer at high speed, beat egg whites with cream of tartar just until stiff peaks form when beaters are slowly raised.

6. In small bowl of electric mixer, using same beaters, beat egg yolks until thick and lemon colored.

7. Add salt, pepper, and milk gradually; beat until well combined.

8. With wire whisk or rubber scraper, using an under-and-over motion, gently fold egg-yolk mixture into egg whites until just combined.

9. Slowly heat a 9- or 10-inch heavy skillet with heat-resistant handle or an omelet pan. To test for proper temperature, sprinkle a little cold water on skillet. Water should sizzle and roll off in drops.

10. Add butter and oil; heat until it sizzles briskly—it should not brown. Tilt pan to coat side with butter mixture.

11. Spread egg mixture evenly in pan; cook, over low heat, without stirring, until lightly browned on underside—about 10 minutes.

12. Transfer skillet to oven. Bake 10 to 12 minutes, or until top seems firm when gently pressed with fingertip.

13. While omelet is baking, add mushrooms, olives, and tomatoes to the sauce. Heat and cook, stirring, until warm.

14. To serve: Fold half of omelet over other half. Remove to heated serv-

ing platter. Pour some of sauce over omelet; pass the rest. Garnish with parsley sprigs.

Makes 4 servings.

Eggs Ranchero I

Sauce
2 tablespoons salad oil
1 cup finely chopped
  green pepper
¼ cup finely
  chopped onion
1 cup chili sauce
1 can (8-ounce size) tomato
  sauce with tomato pieces
2 tablespoons lemon juice

1 teaspoon
  Worcestershire sauce
¼ teaspoon chili powder

Salad oil
6 tortillas
2 tablespoons butter
6 eggs
¼ cup grated sharp
  Cheddar cheese

1. Make sauce: In hot oil in medium saucepan, sauté green pepper and onion until just tender. Add chili sauce, tomato sauce, lemon juice, Worcestershire, and chili powder. Bring to boiling; reduce heat, and simmer, covered and stirring occasionally, 15 minutes.

2. Meanwhile, heat ½-inch salad oil in small skillet until very hot. Fry tortillas, one at a time, 15 seconds on each side. Do not let them become crisp. Drain on paper towels. Place the tortillas in a single layer in heated shallow serving dish.

3. In hot butter in large skillet, fry eggs to desired doneness—3 to 4 minutes.

4. To serve: Top each tortilla with a little sauce, then with a fried egg. Spoon remaining sauce around eggs; sprinkle with cheese. If desired, garnish with thin slices of green pepper. Serve immediately.

Makes 6 servings.

Eggs Ranchero II

Sauce
¼ cup finely chopped onion
1 cup finely chopped
  green pepper
1 cup chili sauce
1 can (8-ounce size)
  tomato sauce
2 tablespoons lemon juice

¼ teaspoon chili powder
1 teaspoon Worcestershire sauce

¼ cup butter
6 eggs
6 minute steaks,
  ¼ inch thick
¼ cup grated sharp
  Cheddar cheese

1. Make sauce: In medium saucepan, combine onion, green pepper, chili sauce, tomato sauce, lemon juice, chili powder, and Worcestershire; bring to boiling. Reduce heat; simmer 15 minutes; stir occasionally.

2. Meanwhile, slowly heat 2 tablespoons butter in large skillet. Break eggs directly into pan; over low heat, sauté eggs gently until of desired doneness—3 to 4 minutes.

3. Meanwhile, in 2 tablespoons hot butter in another large skillet, sauté steaks quickly, about 3 minutes on each side, or until nicely browned.

4. To serve: Top each steak with some of sauce, then with an egg. Sprinkle each egg with some of the cheese.

Makes 6 servings.

Sweet-Red-Pepper Omelets

Filling	Omelets
2 tablespoons butter, melted	6 eggs
½ cup coarsely chopped sweet red peppers	½ teaspoon salt
½ cup coarsely chopped onion	2 tablespoons cold water
¼ teaspoon seasoned salt	2 tablespoons butter
1 tablespoon chopped fresh parsley	

1. Make filling: In hot butter in small skillet, sauté peppers and onion 2 minutes. Cook, covered, over low heat, 5 minutes, or until tender. Stir in seasoned salt and parsley. Set aside until ready to use.

2. Make omelets: In large bowl, with wire whisk or rotary beater, beat eggs with salt and cold water just until well mixed. (Mixture should not be too frothy.)

3. Meanwhile, slowly heat a 9-inch heavy skillet with a heat-resistant handle or omelet pan. To test temperature, sprinkle a small amount of cold water on skillet; water should sizzle and roll off in drops.

4. Add butter; heat until it sizzles briskly—it should not brown.

5. Quickly pour half of egg mixture into skillet; cook over medium heat.

6. As omelet sets, run a spatula around edge to loosen. Tilt pan to let uncooked portion run underneath. Continue loosening and tilting until omelet is almost dry on top and golden brown underneath.

7. Spread omelet with half of filling. To turn out: Loosen edge with spatula. Fold, in thirds, to edge of pan. Tilt out on warm plate. Keep warm.

8. Make a second omelet with rest of egg mixture. Spread with rest of filling. Tilt out on warm plate. Garnish with chopped parsley, if desired. Makes 4 servings.

Eggs Mexicana

3 slices bacon	½ teaspoon chili powder
2 tablespoons butter	1 can (1-pound size) tomatoes,
¼ cup finely chopped	drained and chopped
green pepper	¼ cup finely chopped
6 eggs	ripe olives
1 teaspoon salt	

1. Sauté bacon until crisp. Drain on paper towels; crumble.

2. In hot butter in medium skillet, sauté green pepper until tender—about 5 minutes.

3. Meanwhile, with rotary beater, beat eggs in small bowl with salt and chili powder. Pour over green pepper in skillet.

4. Cook, stirring occasionally, until eggs are partially but not quite set—about 3 minutes.

5. Add tomatoes and olives; cook, stirring, until eggs are set—about 3 minutes longer. Top with bacon.

Makes 3 or 4 servings.

Olive Omelet

6 eggs	¼ cup sliced, pitted
¼ teaspoon chili powder	ripe olives
1 teaspoon salt	2 tablespoons finely chopped
2 tablespoons cold water	pimientos
1 tablespoon olive oil	2 tablespoons finely chopped
	green pepper

1. In medium bowl, with rotary beater or wire whisk, beat eggs with chili powder, salt, and cold water just until well combined, not frothy.

2. Meanwhile, slowly heat oil in a 9-inch heavy skillet with a heat-resistant handle or an omelet pan.

3. Add olives, pimiento, and green pepper to eggs; mix well. Turn mixture into skillet.

4. As eggs set, run spatula under edge to loosen, tilting pan to let uncooked portion run underneath. Continue cooking until bottom is golden brown and eggs are just set.

5. Run under broiler, 6 inches from heat, until top is golden—about 2 minutes.

6. Lift out onto serving platter; do not fold. Cut into pie-shaped wedges.

Makes 4 servings.

SEAFOOD

Seafood Salad

½ pound lobster tail, cooked
½ pound shrimp, cooked
3 pimientos, coarsely chopped
2 hard-cooked eggs,
   coarsely chopped
1 small onion, coarsely
   chopped
1 stalk celery, sliced
¼ cup sherry
2 tablespoons olive oil
2 tablespoons vinegar
¼ teaspoon salt

Dressing
½ cup olive oil
¼ cup vinegar
1 tablespoon mayonnaise
1 pimiento, finely chopped
2 tablespoons finely chopped
   onion
1 hard-cooked egg, finely
   chopped
12 capers, finely chopped
¼ teaspoon salt

Crisp lettuce
Lemon slices
Chopped parsley

1. Cut the lobster meat and the shrimp into small pieces. Place in a medium bowl with the pimientos, eggs, onion, and celery. Combine sherry, 2 tablespoons olive oil, 2 tablespoons vinegar, and ¼ teaspoon salt. Pour over the fish mixture. Toss, to mix well. Refrigerate for several hours.

2. Make dressing: In jar with tight-fitting lid, combine all ingredients for dressing. Shake well. Refrigerate.

3. To serve: Line bowl or individual plates with lettuce. Mound seafood mixture in center. Garnish with the lemon slices, sprinkled lightly with chopped parsley. Pass dressing.

Makes 6 servings.

Rice with Clams and Shrimp

1 dozen small clams,
   in shell

2 pounds shrimp,
   shelled and deveined

4 tablespoons olive oil
1 tablespoon butter
1 cup raw long-grain
   white rice
1 teaspoon salt
1 bay leaf
1 chicken-bouillon cube
2 cloves garlic,
   finely chopped
2 medium onions, peeled
   and finely chopped

2 green peppers, seeded
   and finely chopped
4 large tomatoes, peeled
½ cup pimiento-stuffed
   olives, sliced
2 teaspoons paprika
⅛ teaspoon cayenne
1½ cup (6 ounces) grated
   sharp Cheddar cheese

1. Prepare fried eggplant (see following recipe).

2. Wash clams and shrimp thoroughly. Place clams in saucepan with 6 cups water; bring to boiling. Add shrimp; cook over high heat, covered, 5 minutes. Remove from heat.

3. Pour off enough shellfish liquid to make 2¼ cups. Set aside clams and shrimp, in remaining broth; keep warm.

4. Heat 2 tablespoons olive oil and the butter in 3-quart saucepan. Add rice, and stir to coat well. Add reserved 2¼ cups liquid, the salt, bay leaf, and bouillon cube. Bring to boiling; lower heat, and simmer, covered and without stirring, 25 minutes.

5. Preheat oven to 375°F. Meanwhile, in 2 tablespoons hot oil in 6-quart Dutch oven, sauté garlic, onion, and green pepper until green pepper is tender—about 10 minutes.

6. Chop 2 tomatoes. Add to sautéed vegetables with olives, paprika, and cayenne; cook 5 minutes longer. Keep warm.

7. Drain shellfish, and add with rice to tomato mixture; stir gently to blend. Turn into paella pan or shallow 4-quart casserole.

8. Slice 2 remaining tomatoes, and arrange around edge of dish alternately with fried eggplant. Sprinkle cheese over top of all. Bake 10 to 15 minutes, or until cheese is melted and bubbly.

Makes 6 to 8 servings.

Fried Eggplant

1 small eggplant
   (1 pound)
2 teaspoons salt

2 eggs, beaten
1 cup dry bread crumbs
Olive oil

1. About 4 hours before cooking, cut eggplant into slices ½ inch thick. Sprinkle with salt. Place in strainer, in bowl, and set aside.

2. When ready to cook, dip each piece of eggplant into beaten egg; then roll in bread crumbs.

3. Heat oil (1 inch deep) in large skillet to 375°F. on deep-frying thermometer.

4. Drop eggplant, several pieces at a time, into hot oil, and cook, turning once, until nicely browned on both sides—about 2 minutes.

5. Lift out with slotted utensils, and drain on paper towels. Keep warm.

Makes 6 to 8 servings.

Fish, Veracruz Style

6 tablespoons olive oil	Salt and pepper to taste
1 can (17-ounce size)	1 onion, finely chopped
tomatoes, chopped	6 to 8 red snapper fillets
1 teaspoon sugar	1 can (4-ounce size)
1 teaspoon chili powder	pimientos, chopped
½ teaspoon allspice	2 tablespoons chopped capers
1 clove garlic, crushed	3 ounces pitted green olives,
½ teaspoon grated orange rind	chopped

1. In a heavy skillet, heat 3 tablespoons of the oil.

2. Combine the tomatoes with the sugar, chili powder, allspice, garlic, orange rind, salt, pepper, and onion, and simmer in oil for about 10 minutes, covered.

3. Coat the baking dish with remaining oil. Put the fish in dish; add pimientos, capers, and olives to the tomato mixture and pour over the fish.

4. Bake at 350°F. for 30 to 35 minutes, or until fish flakes easily when pierced with a fork.

Makes 6 servings.

Fish in Orange Juice

8 fish fillets	1½ tablespoons finely chopped
Salt and pepper to taste	green pepper
Juice of 2 limes	½ cup orange juice
4 tablespoons olive oil	
1½ tablespoons finely	3 tablespoons capers
chopped onion	2 oranges, unpeeled and
2 tomatoes,	thinly sliced
peeled and chopped	½ cup toasted, blanched
	almonds, chopped

1. Season fish with salt and pepper, and place in lime juice for 20 minutes.

2. Grease baking pan with half the oil and place fish in pan. Top fish with onion, tomatoes, and green pepper. Pour on the rest of the oil.

3. Place in a 350°F. oven. Bake 15 minutes; then pour over it the orange juice. Cook another 15 to 20 minutes, or until fish flakes easily when lifted with a fork.

4. Garnish with capers, orange slices, and almonds.

Makes 6 to 8 servings.

Cold Fish with Avocado Sauce

6 to 8 fish fillets	2 teaspoons chili powder
Salt and pepper to taste	2½ tablespoons minced
1 tablespoon dried tarragon	fresh parsley
¼ cup lime juice	1 clove garlic, crushed
1 tablespoon butter	1 tablespoon olive oil
2 tomatoes, peeled	
and chopped	Pitted black olives, sliced
3 ripe avocados, mashed	4 ounces pimientos, sliced
2 tablespoons finely	
chopped onion	

1. Preheat oven to 375°F. Season fish with salt, pepper, and tarragon, and soak in lime juice for 20 minutes.

2. Bake fish in buttered baking dish for 25 minutes, or until fish flakes easily when lifted with a fork.

3. While fish is baking, combine the tomatoes, avocado, onion, chili powder, parsley, garlic, oil, and additional salt and pepper. When fish is done, cool, then refrigerate for at least 4 hours, or until thoroughly chilled. Then spread avocado mixture on it.

4. Garnish with olive and pimiento slices.

Makes 6 servings.

Fish in Nut Sauce

6 fish fillets	¼ cup milk
Salt and pepper to taste	¼ cup sweet cream
6 teaspoons lemon juice	1 cup grated mild
1 tablespoon butter	Cheddar cheese
¼ cup melted butter	Dash of cinnamon
¼ cup ground almonds	¼ cup dry bread crumbs

1. Sprinkle fish with salt and pepper and place in the lemon juice for 20 minutes.

2. Remove and place in buttered baking dish. Brush fish with butter.

3. Preheat oven to 450°F. Mix the nuts, milk, cream, and grated cheese, and pour over the fish. Sprinkle with additional salt and pepper, cinnamon, and bread crumbs.

4. Bake for about 30 minutes, or until fish flakes easily when lifted with a fork.

Makes 6 servings.

Meat & Poultry

he Spanish colonialists, finding that Mexico was well suited to stock
raising, quickly introduced cattle, pigs, and sheep to the country. Today
in the north there are vast cattle ranches that provide the meat and
cheese for most of the country, and it is here that most Mexican meat
dishes have originated. It was in the north too that the controversial
chili con carne was invented. Some Mexicans say it is not really their dish
at all but rather a combination developed in Texas. Others says it was
developed in Texas when Texas was part of Mexico and that therefore
the dish is indeed Mexican.

Samples of some of the most famous Mexican dishes, such as enchiladas
and tacos, are included here, as well as a number of excellent barbecue
dishes, such as barbecued spareribs, barbecued sirloin, and barbecued
chicken. Although the Spanish introduced beef and pork to Mexico, the
Mexican Indians introduced barbecuing to the Spanish. The Indians
used to dip their wild meats in spicy sauces, spread them on a wooden
frame made of green sticks, and grill the meat above an open fire. Sliced
into thin strips and cooked slowly, exposed to the smoke of the wood fire
below which was constantly enhanced by the dripping fats, meat cooked
in a *barbacoa* was delicious, and the Spanish quickly copied the custom.

Poultry is very popular in Mexico, whether as an ingredient in enchiladas, in paella, or cooked by itself. Turkey is of course almost a national dish. It was a favorite of Montezuma's, and the most classic Mexican sauce is used to make the country's exquisite turkey mole.

MEAT

Beef Enchiladas

Meat Filling
1 pound ground chuck
1 clove garlic,
   finely chopped
2 teaspoons salt
1 tablespoon wine vinegar
1 tablespoon tequila,
   cognac, or water
1 tablespoon chili powder
1 can (1-pound size)
   kidney beans, undrained

2 tablespoons flour
2 cans (10½-ounce size)
   tomato purée
1 tablespoon wine vinegar
1 beef-bouillon cube
1 cup boiling water
2 tablespoons finely
   chopped green chilies
Dash ground cumin
½ teaspoon salt
Dash pepper

Tomato Sauce
3 tablespoons salad oil
1 clove garlic,
   very finely chopped
¼ cup chopped onion

Enchiladas
10 frozen tortillas
1 cup grated sharp Cheddar
   cheese or 1 cup cubed
   Monterey Jack cheese

1. Prepare meat filling: In medium skillet over low heat, sauté chuck with garlic, salt, vinegar, tequila, and chili powder until chuck is browned. Then stir in kidney beans. Set aside.

2. Make tomato sauce: In hot oil in skillet, sauté garlic and onion until golden—about 5 minutes. Remove from heat. Stir in flour until smooth; then stir in tomato purée, vinegar, and bouillon cube (dissolved in boiling water). Bring mixture to boiling point, stirring over medium heat. Add green chilies, cumin, salt, and pepper; simmer, uncovered and stirring occasionally, about 5 minutes. Set aside.

3. To assemble enchiladas: Preheat oven to 350°F. Place about ⅓ cup filling in center of each tortilla; roll up; arrange, seam side down, in a 13-by-9-by-2-inch baking dish. Pour tomato sauce over all; sprinkle with cheese; bake 25 minutes.

Makes 10 enchiladas, or 5 servings.

Note: Meat filling and tomato sauce may be made ahead of time and refrigerated. Reheat slightly when ready to use.

Chili and Enchiladas

Chili con Carne
2 tablespoons salad oil
1 cup chopped onion
3 pounds ground chuck
2 packages chili-
seasoning mix or
4 tablespoons chili powder
1 can (1-pound-12-ounce
size) tomatoes
1 cup red wine
2 cans (1-pound size)
red kidney beans,
undrained

Enchiladas
12 frozen tortillas
3 cups (¾ pound)
grated sharp Cheddar cheese
1 cup chopped onion

Sauce
1 can (15-ounce size)
tomato sauce with
tomato bits
2 tablespoons chopped
green chilies

1. Make chili con carne: In hot oil in large skillet, sauté 1 cup chopped onion until golden—about 5 minutes. Remove to small bowl.

2. In same skillet, over high heat, cook meat, stirring occasionally, until browned—about 15 minutes.

3. Stir in sautéed onion, chili-seasoning mix, and tomatoes. Bring to boiling; reduce heat; simmer, covered and stirring occasionally, 45 minutes. Add wine; simmer, uncovered, 20 minutes longer, or until mixture is slightly thickened.

4. Spoon into 4-quart, shallow ovenproof serving dish. Stir in undrained kidney beans.

5. Make enchiladas: Heat tortillas as package label directs. Preheat oven to 350°F.

6. In medium bowl, combine 2 cups grated cheese and the onion. Place a rounded tablespoon of cheese mixture on each tortilla. Roll up. Arrange, seam side down, on chili in serving dish.

7. Combine tomato sauce and chopped green chilies; spoon over tortillas. Sprinkle with remaining cheese.

8. Bake 30 to 35 minutes, or until sauce bubbles and cheese melts.
Makes 8 servings.
Note: Chili con carne may be made early in the day through step 4, and refrigerated. Remove from refrigerator while preheating oven, and continue with step 5.

Red Peppers Stuffed with Chili con Carne

6 red peppers (2½ pounds)	1 can (1-pound size) tomatoes, undrained
1 tablespoon salt	1 can (15-ounce size) kidney beans, undrained
Chili con Carne	1½ tablespoons chili powder
2 tablespoons salad oil	1½ teaspoons salt
4 cups cubed, cooked roast beef (1½ pounds)	1½ teaspoons dried oregano leaves
1 cup sliced onion	½ teaspoon dried basil leaves
1 clove garlic, crushed	⅓ cup red wine

1. Wash peppers. Cut ½-inch-thick slice from top of each. Scoop out seeds and ribs.

2. In large kettle, bring 4 quarts water and 1 tablespoon salt to boiling. Add peppers; reduce heat, and simmer, uncovered, 10 minutes, or just until peppers are tender. Drain.

3. Meanwhile, make chili con carne: In hot oil in skillet, sauté beef, onion, and garlic until onion is tender—about 5 minutes.

4. Add tomatoes, kidney beans, chili powder, salt, oregano, and basil; bring to boiling. Reduce heat, and simmer, uncovered, 20 minutes. Preheat oven to 350°F.

5. Add wine to chili; simmer, uncovered, 15 minutes longer.

6. Fill peppers with chili. Place in shallow baking dish.

7. Bake, covered, 10 to 15 minutes, or until heated through.

Makes 6 servings.

Upside-Down Chili Pie

1 tablespoon salad oil	½ cup red wine
1½ pounds ground chuck	1 package (12-ounce size) corn-muffin mix
½ cup chopped onion	1 can (8¾-ounce size) cream-style corn
1 clove garlic, crushed	1 egg
1 tablespoon chili powder	¼ cup milk
1¼ teaspoons salt	
1 teaspoon dried oregano leaves	2 tablespoons grated sharp Cheddar cheese
½ teaspoon dried basil leaves	1 tablespoon chopped fresh parsley
1 can (8¼-ounce size) tomatoes, undrained	1 tablespoon ketchup
1 can (8½-ounce size) kidney beans, undrained	

1. In hot oil in heavy, 10-inch skillet, sauté chuck, onion, and garlic until chuck is browned—about 5 minutes.

2. Add chili powder, salt, oregano, basil, and tomatoes; mix well. Cook over low heat, covered, 30 minutes. Stir in kidney beans and wine; cook 10 minutes longer.

3. Preheat oven to 400°F.

4. In medium bowl, combine corn-muffin mix, corn, egg, and milk; mix only until muffin mix is moistened.

5. Skim excess fat from meat mixture in skillet, and discard. Pour muffin mix over meat mixture, spreading evenly.

6. Bake 25 minutes, or until top is golden brown. Let stand in skillet 2 minutes; then invert onto serving platter. Garnish with grated cheese and parsley. Serve with ketchup.

Makes 8 servings.

Chili

1½ pounds ground chuck	2 cans (15-ounce size) kidney beans, undrained
¼ cup chopped onion	
1¼ teaspoons salt	1 can (1-pound size) tomatoes, drained
Dash pepper	
½ tablespoon salad oil	6 hamburger buns, toasted (optional)
1 package chili-seasoning mix, or 2 tablespoons chili powder	

1. In medium bowl, combine chuck, onion, salt, and pepper; mix lightly with fork until well combined. Shape into 6 patties about ¾ inch thick.

2. In hot oil in large skillet, sauté patties until nicely browned on each side—about 4 minutes a side. Remove from heat; lift out patties, and set aside.

3. Drain off drippings; return 1 tablespoon to skillet. Sprinkle chili-seasoning mix over drippings in skillet. Gradually stir in kidney beans and tomatoes.

4. Bring to boiling; reduce heat. Return beef patties to skillet; simmer, covered, 15 minutes.

5. May be served on toasted hamburger buns.

Makes 6 servings.

Mexican Meatballs with Chili Sauce

Meatballs
3 fresh white-bread slices
¼ cup milk
1 pound ground chuck
1 pound ground pork
2 teaspoons salt
¼ teaspoon pepper
1 teaspoon chili powder
½ teaspoon dried
   oregano leaves
2 eggs, slightly beaten

Chili Sauce
2 tablespoons olive oil
½ cup finely chopped onion
1 clove garlic, crushed
1½ tablespoons chili powder
1 teaspoon salt
¼ teaspoon dried
   oregano leaves
¼ teaspoon ground cumin
1 can (10½-ounce size)
   tomato purée
1 cup water

1. Make meatballs: In medium bowl, soak bread slices in milk.

2. Mash bread slices with fork. Add remaining meatball ingredients; mix well with hands to combine.

3. With moistened hands, shape mixture into meatballs, 1½ inches in diameter. Set aside.

4. Make chili sauce: In hot oil in medium saucepan, sauté onion and garlic, stirring, until golden—about 5 minutes.

5. Add rest of sauce ingredients; mix well. Bring mixture to boiling, stirring. Reduce heat; simmer, covered, 15 minutes, or until sauce has thickened.

6. Add 1 cup water to sauce; return to boiling. Drop in meatballs, one by one.

7. Simmer, covered, 35 minutes, stirring occasionally. Serve over hot corn-bread squares, if desired.

Makes 6 to 8 servings.

Chili-Tortilla Pie

8 frankfurters
2 cans (15- or 15½-ounce
   size) chili con carne
   with beans
1 can (12-ounce size)
   whole-kernel corn
   with peppers

¼ cup pitted olives, halved
2 cans (8-ounce size)
   tomato sauce with onions
12 frozen tortillas, thawed
½ cup grated sharp Cheddar
   cheese

1. Heat oven to 400°F.

2. Slice frankfurters in rounds, ½ inch thick. In medium saucepan, combine frankfurters, chili, corn, olives, and 1½ cans tomato sauce. Bring to boiling, stirring.

3. Cut tortillas into quarters. Cover bottom of a shallow, 1½-quart casserole with 6 tortilla pieces. Spoon about ¾ cup of chili mixture over tortillas; repeat, layering tortillas and chili mixture until all are used; end with chili. Sprinkle cheese over top. Add rest of tomato sauce.

4. Bake, uncovered, 20 minutes, or until cheese starts to brown. Makes 5 to 6 servings.

Casserole Mexicana

1 tablespoon salad oil	1 can (3½-ounce size)
½ pound ground chuck	pitted black olives
1 envelope taco, chili, or	1 package (6½-ounce size)
sloppy joe seasoning mix	tortilla chips
1 can (1-pound-4-ounce size)	¼ cup grated sharp
kidney beans, undrained	Cheddar cheese
1 can (8-ounce size)	
tomato sauce	

1. Preheat oven to 350°F.

2. Heat salad oil in a large skillet. Add ground chuck, and sauté until browned. Stir in the seasoning mix, then the kidney beans and the tomato sauce. Bring to boiling, stirring often. Pour meat mixture into 2-quart casserole.

3. Drain olives, and sprinkle over top of meat mixture. Arrange about half of the tortilla chips around edge; then sprinkle cheese on chips.

4. Bake casserole 10 minutes, or until the cheese is melted. Makes 6 servings.

Tamale Pie

¼ cup salad oil	1½ tablespoons chili powder
2 cups finely chopped onion	4 teaspoons dried
1 clove garlic, crushed	oregano leaves
1½ pounds ground chuck	1½ tablespoons salt
¾ pound ground pork	1 cup pitted ripe olives, drained
sausage	1¾ cups yellow corn meal
1 can (1-pound size)	2⅓ cups cold water
stewed tomatoes	1 egg, well beaten
1 can (12-ounce size)	1⅔ cups grated sharp
corn with peppers, drained	Cheddar cheese
1 can (8-ounce size)	
tomato sauce	

1. In hot oil in large skillet or Dutch oven, sauté onion and garlic until tender—about 5 minutes.

2. Add the chuck and the sausage; sauté, stirring, until they are well browned.

3. Remove from heat; pour off excess fat. Add tomatoes, corn, tomato sauce, chili powder, oregano, 1 tablespoon salt, and the olives (except 6—reserve for garnish); mix well. Set aside.

4. Preheat oven to 350°F.

5. In medium saucepan, combine corn meal and remaining salt with water and the egg. Cook, stirring, over low heat, until thickened (spoon will leave a path when pulled through mixture). Stir in 1 cup cheese.

6. Layer one-third corn meal mixture over bottom of shallow, 3-quart casserole. Cover with meat mixture.

7. Spoon rest of corn meal mixture around top edge of casserole, leaving a small opening in center.

8. Sprinkle the remaining cheese over corn meal edge. Then place the reserved olives around inside edge of corn meal.

9. Bake 30 minutes, or until golden brown on top.
Makes 8 servings.

Tamales with Pork

Filling
1 pound ground pork
1 tablespoon salad oil
1 teaspoon salt
Dash pepper
Dash ground coriander
1 can (8-ounce size)
    tomato sauce

Corn Meal
2 cups yellow corn meal
3 cups cold water
2 teaspoons salt
¼ cup butter
2 eggs

1. Make filling: In medium skillet, fry pork in hot oil until pink color disappears. Add remaining ingredients, and stir over moderate heat until most of liquid is absorbed—about 5 minutes.

2. Make corn meal: Stir corn meal into cold water in medium saucepan. Cook over low heat, stirring constantly, until thick—about 5 minutes. Remove from heat. Add salt and butter; cool 3 to 5 minutes. Vigorously beat eggs into corn-meal mixture.

3. To assemble: Tear off four 6-inch squares of foil. Place large spoonful of corn-meal mixture on each square. Hollow slightly with back of spoon. Divide meat mixture and place into hollows; top with remaining corn meal. Fold foil to form rectangular packages.

4. Place on rack in large kettle over boiling water. Cover kettle, and steam 40 minutes. Serve with sauce for chilies rellenos (see p. 28).
Makes 4 servings.

Beef Tacos with Green Chili Salsa

Filling
1 pound ground chuck
1 medium onion, chopped
1 clove garlic, crushed
2 tablespoons soy sauce
1 tablespoon Worcestershire sauce
1 can (8-ounce size) tomato sauce

Salad oil for deep-frying
12 tortillas
1 medium tomato, coarsely chopped (1 cup)
1 cup shredded lettuce
1 cup grated sharp Cheddar cheese

1. Make filling: In hot skillet, sauté chuck with onion until meat loses red color. Add garlic, soy sauce, Worcestershire, and tomato sauce; simmer about 10 minutes. Keep warm.

2. In heavy saucepan, slowly heat salad oil (at least 3 inches) to 420°F. on deep-frying thermometer.

3. Gently drop a tortilla into hot oil; when it rises to top, grasp it with two tongs, and bend it into a U shape. Hold in oil until crisp—about 2 minutes. Remove, and drain on paper towels. Continue until the tortillas are used, frying one at a time.

4. Preheat oven to 400°F.

5. In each tortilla, arrange, in order, a layer of filling, a little chopped tomato, a small mound of shredded lettuce, and some grated cheese. Place in shallow baking dish.

6. Bake, uncovered, 10 minutes, or just until cheese melts. Serve with green-chili salsa (see following recipe).
Makes 6 servings.

Green-Chili Salsa

1½ cups peeled, chopped tomato
1 cup chopped Bermuda onion
2 green chilies, chopped

2 cloves garlic, crushed
½ teaspoon salt
½ teaspoon monosodium glutamate

1. In medium bowl, combine all ingredients; mix well.

2. Let stand about 15 minutes, to develop flavor, before serving.
Makes about 2½ cups.

Rancho Grande Steak

4-pound top-round steak,	1 teaspoon salt
2 inches thick	½ teaspoon pepper
⅔ cup red wine	½ teaspoon dried
3 tablespoons lemon juice	rosemary leaves
2 tablespoons salad oil	

1. Wipe steak with damp paper towels.

2. In shallow pan, combine wine, lemon juice, salad oil, salt, pepper, and rosemary; stir until well blended. Place steak in marinade. With fork, pierce all surfaces thoroughly and deeply. Let stand 15 minutes; turn several times.

3. Preheat electric skillet to 400°F.

4. Remove steak from marinade. Brown both sides of steak in hot skillet—about 5 minutes a side.

5. Reduce skillet temperature to 325°F. Continue cooking about 15 minutes on each side for rare.

6. To serve: Slice meat thinly on the diagonal, across the grain.
Makes 8 to 10 servings.

Barbecued Sirloin

2-pound sirloin steak,	1 teaspoon chili powder
1¼ inches thick	1 teaspoon dried
⅓ cup dark rum	oregano leaves
1 large clove garlic, crushed	Dash Tabasco

1. Wipe meat with damp paper towels.

2. In shallow pan, combine rum, garlic, chili powder, oregano, and Tabasco; stir until well blended. Place meat in marinade. Let stand 15 minutes; turn twice.

3. Remove meat from marinade; reserve marinade. Place meat on grill, set 2 to 3 inches above prepared coals. Grill, basting frequently with marinade and turning occasionally, 10 to 14 minutes for rare.

4. To serve: Slice meat thinly on the diagonal, across the grain.
Makes 6 servings.

To cook indoors: Broil 8 minutes; turn; brush with marinade; broil 8 minutes longer for rare.

Hamburgers Ranchero

Hamburgers
2 pounds ground chuck
⅓ cup water
1 teaspoon salt
¼ teaspoon pepper

3 slices bacon, diced
1 cup finely chopped
   green pepper
¼ cup finely chopped onion

1 can (8-ounce size)
   tomato sauce
1 cup chili sauce
2 tablespoons lemon juice
1 teaspoon
   Worcestershire sauce
¼ teaspoon chili powder

8 eggs
¼ cup butter

1. Make hamburgers: In large bowl, combine chuck, ⅓ cup water, the salt, and pepper; mix lightly with fork. Shape into 8 patties ¾ inch thick.

2. In large skillet, sauté bacon until crisp. Remove with slotted spoon; drain on paper towels. Reserve for garnish. In hot drippings, brown hamburgers on each side; then remove.

3. In same skillet, sauté green pepper and onion until tender—about 5 minutes. Stir in tomato sauce, chili sauce, lemon juice, Worcestershire, and chili powder. Return hamburgers to pan. Simmer, uncovered, 30 minutes.

4. About 5 minutes before serving, in another large skillet, fry eggs in hot butter to desired doneness. (Or poach eggs, if preferred.)

5. To serve: Arrange hamburgers with sauce on serving platter. Top each with an egg; sprinkle with reserved bacon.

Makes 8 servings.

Mexican Pork Chops

Meat
8 rib pork chops,
   1 inch thick
½ teaspoon chili powder
¼ cup salad oil
2 cloves garlic, crushed
1 cup coarsely
   chopped onion
4 to 6 Italian sausages
   (½ to ¾ pound)
2 teaspoons salt
¼ teaspoon pepper

1 can (8-ounce size)
   tomato sauce
1 can (10½-ounce size)
   condensed beef consomme,
   undiluted

Pepper Sauce
¼ cup salad oil
2 cups sliced onion
3 medium green peppers
   cut in ¼-inch-thick rings
1 teaspoon seasoned salt

2 tablespoons flour   3 medium tomatoes,
¼ cup water   cut in wedges

1. Wipe pork chops with damp paper towels. Trim off fat, if necessary. Sprinkle chops lightly on each side with chili powder.

2. In ¼ cup hot oil in Dutch oven, brown chops well on both sides— about 20 minutes in all. Remove chops, and set aside.

3. In drippings in Dutch oven, sauté garlic, chopped onion, and sausage until sausage is golden brown—about 5 minutes.

4. Add salt, pepper, tomato sauce, and consommé; bring to boiling, stirring. Add browned chops; reduce heat, and simmer, covered, 50 minutes, or until tender.

5. About 15 minutes before chops are done, make pepper sauce: In ¼ cup hot oil in large skillet, sauté sliced onion and green pepper 5 minutes. Sprinkle with seasoned salt; cook, covered, 5 minutes longer.

6. Arrange chops and sausage on heated platter. Keep warm.

7. Spoon off fat from drippings in Dutch oven (drippings should measure about 1¼ cups). Mix flour with water until smooth. Gradually stir into drippings; cook, stirring, until boiling and thickened.

8. To serve: Pour gravy over chops. Then spread with pepper sauce. Garnish with tomato wedges.

Makes 8 servings.

Barbecued Spareribs

Meat   ¼ cup chili sauce
4½ pounds spareribs   1 can (8-ounce size)
1 onion, peeled   tomato sauce with tomato bits
   and quartered   ¼ cup chopped onion
2 teaspoons salt   2 tablespoons brown sugar
¼ teaspoon pepper   1 tablespoon
1 bay leaf   Worcestershire sauce
1 quart water   1 teaspoon dry mustard

Barbecue Sauce
⅓ cup cider vinegar

1. Place ribs, onion quarters, salt, pepper, bay leaf, and 1 quart water in large kettle. Bring to boiling; reduce heat, and simmer, covered, 1¼ hours, or until tender. Drain; pat spareribs dry with paper towels.

2. Meanwhile, make barbecue sauce: In medium saucepan, combine

all sauce ingredients. Bring to boiling; reduce heat, and simmer, uncovered and stirring occasionally, 30 minutes.

3. Place spareribs on grill, set about 5 inches above prepared coals. Grill 5 minutes on each side, or until browned; brush with some sauce. Grill, brushing several times with sauce and turning occasionally, 20 minutes longer. Cut into serving-size pieces.

Makes 6 servings.

To cook indoors: After drying spareribs with paper towels, arrange in shallow pan. Broil, 6 inches from heat, about 5 minutes on each side, or until browned. Then brush with sauce, and broil 7 minutes on each side.

Broiled Leg-of-Lamb Slices with Sauce Maître d'Hôtel

7-pound leg of lamb, boned	1 teaspoon dried oregano leaves
	½ teaspoon dried
Marinade	basil leaves
½ cup salad oil	¼ teaspoon pepper
¼ cup lemon juice	2 bay leaves
1 teaspoon salt	2 cloves garlic, crushed

1. Place leg of lamb fat side down. With sharp knife, make gashes in thick sections of lamb, to make it as uniformly thick as possible.

2. Remove excess fat. Wipe lamb with damp paper towels. Place in large, shallow baking dish.

3. Make marinade: In jar with tight-fitting lid, combine all marinade ingredients; shake vigorously to combine. Pour over lamb.

4. Refrigerate, covered, overnight; turn lamb occasionally.

5. Adjust grill 5 inches above prepared coals. Remove lamb from marinade; lay flat on grill, fat side up.

6. Grill lamb 40 to 50 minutes, turning and basting several times with marinade. Test for doneness by making small cut in thickest part with sharp knife.

7. To serve: Remove to carving board or heated serving platter. Slice, at a slight angle, into ¼-inch-thick slices. Serve with sauce maître d'hôtel.

Makes 8 servings.

To cook indoors: Place meat, fat side down, on broiler rack; broil, 4 inches from heat, 20 minutes. Turn with tongs; brush with marinade; broil 25 to 30 minutes longer, or until of desired doneness.

Sauce Maître d'Hôtel

¼ cup butter	1½ tablespoons chopped
¼ cup finely chopped onion	parsley
¼ cup unsifted all-	1½ tablespoons chopped
purpose flour	fresh tarragon leaves, **or**
1 teaspoon salt	1½ teaspoons dried tarragon
Dash cayenne	leaves
2 cups milk	2 eggs yolks, beaten
⅓ cup lemon juice	

1. In hot butter in medium saucepan, sauté onion 3 minutes. Remove from heat. Stir in flour, salt, and cayenne. Gradually stir in milk.

2. Bring to boiling; reduce heat, and simmer 5 minutes, stirring occasionally.

3. Stir in lemon juice, parsley, and tarragon.

4. Stir some of hot mixture into egg yolks, combining well. Return to saucepan; heat slightly.

Makes about 2½ cups.

Veal Scallops in Olive-Wine Sauce

6 veal scallops	⅓ cup salad oil
(about 2 pounds)	1 cup thinly sliced onion
⅓ cup unsifted all-	2 cups white wine
purpose flour	1½ cups thickly sliced,
1 teaspoon salt	pitted jumbo ripe olives
¼ teaspoon pepper	

1. Wipe veal scallops with damp paper towels; dry well on paper towels.

2. Combine flour, salt, and pepper; mix well. Use to coat veal scallops well on each side.

3. Slowly heat oil in large skillet. Over medium heat, sauté veal until golden brown on each side.

4. Put veal to one side. Add onion, and sauté until tender—about 5 minutes.

5. Add wine and sliced olives; simmer, covered, over medium heat, for 15 minutes, or until the veal scallops are tender.

Makes 4 to 6 servings.

POULTRY

Chicken Enchiladas with Red Chili Sauce

Enchiladas
Salad oil for frying
12 frozen tortillas
1 cup light cream
2 chicken-bouillon cubes

Filling
2 tablespoons salad oil
1 medium onion,
   finely chopped
2 green chilies,
   finely chopped

1 clove garlic, crushed
1 can (1-pound size)
   tomato purée
2 cups chopped cooked
   chicken
½ teaspoon salt
Dash pepper

½ pound Cheddar
   cheese, finely grated

1. Make red chili sauce (see following recipe). Keep warm.
2. Heat ½-inch salad oil in small skillet until very hot. Fry tortillas one at a time, 15 seconds on each side. Do not let them become crisp. Drain on paper towels. Set aside.
3. In small saucepan, heat cream with bouillon cubes until cubes are dissolved. Keep warm.
4. Make filling: In hot oil in large skillet, sauté onion until tender—about 5 minutes. Add green chilies, garlic, tomato purée, chicken, salt, and pepper; simmer, uncovered, 10 minutes.
5. Preheat oven to 350°F.
6. Dip each tortilla in cream mixture. Top each with heaping table-spoonful of filling; roll up. Place, seam side down, in a greased 3-quart shallow baking dish. Pour red chili sauce over tortillas; sprinkle with cheese.
7. Bake, uncovered, 15 minutes.
Makes 4 servings.

Red Chili Sauce

2 tablespoons shortening
3 to 4 tablespoons
   chili powder
2 tablespoons flour
¾ teaspoon salt

½ teaspoon garlic salt
Pinch oregano
Pinch cumin
2 cups water

1. Melt shortening in medium skillet. Add chili powder, flour, salt, garlic salt, oregano, and cumin; stir until well blended. Gradually stir in water.

2. Bring to boiling, stirring constantly; reduce heat, and simmer 10 minutes.

Makes 1⅔ cups.

Hickory Barbecued Chicken

2 2½-pound broiler- fryers, quartered	1 clove garlic, crushed
	2 tablespoons lemon juice
	1 tablespoon
Marinade	Worcestershire sauce
½ cup salad oil	1 teaspoon salt
½ cup hickory-flavored	⅛ teaspoon pepper
ketchup	

1. Wash chicken; pat dry with paper towels. Arrange in single layer in baking pan.

2. Make marinade: In small bowl, combine all marinade ingredients; mix well. Pour over chicken.

3. Refrigerate, covered, about 2 hours; turn chicken occasionally.

4. Remove chicken from marinade; reserve marinade.

5. Place chicken, skin side up, on grill set about 5 inches above the prepared coals. Grill, turning and basting frequently with marinade, 50 to 60 minutes. Heat any remaining marinade at edge of grill, and serve over chicken.

Makes 6 servings.

To cook indoors: Place chicken in broiler pan with rack. Broil, 6 inches from heat, turning and basting frequently with marinade, about 45 minutes.

Oven-Barbecued Chicken with Olive Sauce

2½- to 3-pound ready-to-
    cook broiler-fryer, cut in
    serving-size pieces
	½ cup chopped pimiento-
	    stuffed olives

	3 tablespoons light-brown sugar
Olive Sauce	1 tablespoon onion, minced
½ cup chili sauce	½ cup water
½ cup cider vinegar	
	Parsley (optional)

1. Preheat oven to 350°F. Rinse chicken; drain well on paper towels.

2. Place chicken, skin side up, in a 13-by-9-by-2-inch baking pan; bake, uncovered, 30 minutes.

3. Meanwhile, make olive sauce: In small saucepan, combine chili sauce with rest of ingredients.

4. Bring to boiling; reduce heat, and simmer 20 minutes, stirring occasionally.

5. Pour sauce over chicken; bake, covered, 15 minutes. Baste with sauce in pan; bake, uncovered, 15 minutes longer.

6. Serve garnished with parsley, if desired.

Makes 4 servings.

Paella

2 2-pound broiler-fryers, cut up	1 teaspoon crumbled saffron
Giblets	½ teaspoon pepper
3 teaspoons salt	1 jar (11½-ounce size) whole clams, undrained, or 8-12 fresh clams
1 carrot, pared and cut into rings	
1 small onion, peeled	1½ cups raw long-grain white rice
2 bay leaves	
2 parsley sprigs	1 can (8-ounce size) artichoke hearts
6 whole black peppers	
3 cups water	2 large tomatoes, coarsely chopped (3 cups)
½ cup olive oil	
4 cloves garlic, peeled and slivered	1 pound cooked shrimp, shelled and deveined
1 large green pepper, cut into strips (2 cups)	2 tablespoons finely chopped parsley

1. Wipe chicken with damp paper towels; set aside.

2. In large saucepan, combine giblets, ½ teaspoon salt, carrot rings, onion, bay leaves, parsley sprigs, black peppers, and water. Bring to boiling; reduce heat, and simmer, covered, 45 minutes.

3. Meanwhile, slowly heat oil in large Dutch oven. In hot oil, slowly brown chicken all over, a few pieces at a time; removing as it browns.

4. In same hot oil, sauté garlic, green pepper, saffron, and pepper, stirring, about 5 minutes. Arrange browned chicken pieces on top. Preheat oven to 350°F.

5. Drain and discard giblets and vegetables, reserving cooking liquid. Add enough liquid from clams to make 3 cups. Add to mixture in oven.

6. Bring to boiling over medium heat. Using fork, stir in rice and rest of salt, mixing well. Bring back to boiling.

7. Bake, covered, 1 hour, stirring rice every 20 minutes.

8. Meanwhile, drain clams; cut in half. Rinse artichokes in cold water; drain well; cut crosswise into 1/4-inch slices. Combine clams, artichokes, tomatoes, and shrimp in large bowl. Add to chicken and rice in Dutch oven, mixing well.

9. Bake 10 minutes longer. Arrange chicken on rice and vegetables; sprinkle with parsley.

Makes 6 to 8 servings.

Mexican Chicken and Rice

2 1½-pound broiler- fryers, split	1 cup water
¼ teaspoon salt	1 package (6-ounce size) Spanish-rice mix
⅛ teaspoon pepper	¼ teaspoon dried
⅛ teaspoon paprika	basil leaves
2 tablespoons salad oil	1 package (10-ounce size)
1 can (1-pound size) stewed tomatoes	frozen green peas

1. Preheat oven to 350°F.

2. Wash chicken; pat dry with paper towels. Turn wing tips under. Sprinkle with salt, pepper, and paprika.

3. In hot oil in large skillet, brown chicken quickly. Remove as browned.

4. To skillet, add stewed tomatoes, water, the seasonings from Spanish-rice mix, the basil, and peas. Bring to boiling, stirring occasionally.

5. Sprinkle rice over bottom of 13-by-9-by-2-inch baking dish. Top with chicken, skin side up. Pour hot tomato mixture over all.

6. Bake, covered, 40 minutes. Remove cover; with a fork, carefully fluff rice well. Bake, uncovered, 10 minutes longer, or until chicken is tender and rice absorbs liquid.

Makes 4 servings.

Turkey Mole

1 6-pound ready-to-cook
  turkey, cut up
1 onion, coarsely chopped
2 stalks celery, cut up
2 teaspoons salt
8 whole black peppers
1 can (10½-ounce size)
  condensed chicken broth,
  undiluted
3 cups water

3 tablespoons salad oil
1 cup sliced onion
1 cup chopped
  green pepper
1 clove garlic, crushed
½ cup toasted
  slivered almonds

¼ cup dark raisins
4 tablespoons toasted
  sesame seeds (see Note)
2 tablespoons sugar
1 tablespoon flour
1½ teaspoons salt
1 teaspoon chili powder
½ teaspoon cinnamon
½ teaspoon ground
  coriander
½ teaspoon cumin seed
⅛ teaspoon ground cloves
⅛ teaspoon pepper
1 square (1-ounce size)
  unsweetened chocolate
1 can (1-pound size)
  tomatoes, undrained

1. Place turkey, chopped onion, the celery, 2 teaspoons salt, the black peppers, chicken broth, and water in a large kettle. Bring to boiling; reduce heat, and simmer, covered, 1½ hours. Remove turkey; drain well. Boil broth rapidly, uncovered, until reduced to 3 cups—about 15 to 20 minutes. Strain, and set aside.

2. In hot oil in large skillet, brown turkey pieces. Place, in a single layer, in a large roasting pan or shallow baking dish.

3. In same skillet, sauté sliced onion, the green pepper, and garlic until tender—about 5 minutes. Add more oil if necessary.

4. In electric blender, combine almonds, raisins, and 3 tablespoons sesame seeds; cover, and blend at high speed until finely ground. Turn into small bowl; stir in sugar, flour, salt, chili powder, cinnamon, coriander, cumin, cloves, and pepper. Stir into sautéed vegetables along with chocolate, tomatoes, and 3 cups reserved broth.

5. Bring to boiling, stirring constantly; reduce heat, and simmer, covered and stirring occasionally, 15 minutes.

6. Preheat oven to 375°F. Spoon sauce over turkey in roasting pan.

7. Bake, covered and basting once or twice with sauce, 1 hour; or until turkey is tender.

8. To serve: Arrange turkey pieces attractively in a shallow serving

dish or deep platter. Pour sauce over turkey pieces; sprinkle with remaining sesame seeds. If desired, garnish with parsley.

Makes 6 to 8 servings.

Note: To toast sesame seeds, place in shallow pan, and bake in 325°F oven about 5 minutes.

Turkey and Ham Paella

½ cup salad oil	1½ cups raw long-grain
1½ cups chopped onion	white rice
1 clove garlic, crushed	1 cup frozen peas
1 can (10½-ounce size)	1 package (9-ounce size)
condensed chicken broth	frozen artichoke hearts
1 bottle (8-ounce size)	3 cups cooked turkey,
clam juice	cut in large pieces
1 can (1-pound size)	½ pound cooked ham,
tomatoes	cut in strips
1 teaspoon salt	
¼ teaspoon pepper	Chopped parsley
¼ teaspoon saffron	

1. Preheat oven to 350°F.

2. In hot oil in large skillet, sauté onion and garlic until onion is golden —about 5 minutes.

3. Stir in undiluted chicken broth, clam juice, tomatoes, salt, pepper, and saffron; bring to boiling, stirring. Stir in rice, peas, and artichoke hearts; return to boiling.

4. Pour into a 2-quart shallow baking dish. Arrange pieces of turkey and ham on the rice mixture.

5. Bake, uncovered, 45 to 55 minutes, or until rice is tender and all liquid is absorbed.

6. To serve: Fluff rice with a fork. Arrange some of the artichoke hearts in center of paella. Sprinkle with chopped parsley.

Makes 6 servings.

Roast Ducklings, Mexican Style

2 4- to 4½-pound	2 cups sweet red wine
ready-to-cook ducklings	1 tablespoon
2 large cooking apples	Worcestershire sauce
2 medium onions	5 drops Tabasco
¼ cup butter	1 teaspoon salt
Paprika	

1. Wash ducklings, inside and out; pat dry with paper towels.

2. Fill each duck cavity with one apple and one onion, each cut in eighths.

3. Secure neck and cavity openings with skewers; tie legs and tail together.

4. Melt butter in electric skillet at 350°F. Brown ducks, one at a time, on all sides. Pour off accumulated fat. Return ducks to skillet. Sprinkle with paprika.

5. Combine wine, Worcestershire, Tabasco, and salt; add to skillet.

6. Simmer, covered, at 225°F. with vent open, 2 hours, or until tender. If more browning and a crisper skin are desired, place ducks on rack of range broiler for 5 minutes.

Makes 8 servings.

Breads, Cakes, & Cookies

The bread of Mexico is the tortilla, a corn-meal pancake made on a griddle. It is sometimes eaten by itself, but usually it is accompanied by spicy sauces which are dipped onto the pancake which is then rolled up and eaten like a curvaceous sandwich. Tortillas are fried or stuffed to make tacos or enchiladas or to form the basis of a casserole. But Mexicans like other breads as well, such as the unusual olive corn-meal bread.

Since lunch is usually the main meal in Mexico, supper is often a light meal composed principally of sweet breads and pastries. As a result, there are innumerable Mexican pastries and baked confections. Among the most famous are *conchas*, or shells, which are a kind of sweet roll, and *churros* and *buñuelos*, which are crispy doughnuts fried in oil and sprinkled with sugar or syrup.

Tortillas

1½ cups yellow corn meal	¾ teaspoon salt
1½ cups unsifted all-purpose flour	3 tablespoons shortening
	¾ cup warm water

1. In large bowl, combine corn meal, flour, and salt. With pastry blender or 2 knives, cut in shortening until well blended. Add warm water

(use more, if necessary), stirring until mixture is completely moistened. Form into a ball.

2. On floured surface, knead or work dough with hands until it is no longer sticky—about 5 minutes. Divide into 2 equal balls. Let rest 20 minutes at room temperature.

3. Then, on floured surface, roll out each ball into 18-inch circle. With paring knife, cut 5 tortillas from each circle (use rim of 5¾-inch mixing bowl as guide).

4. On heated, ungreased griddle, bake tortillas 1 minute; turn, and bake 1 minute longer.

Makes 10.

Olive-Corn-Meal Bread

6 slices bacon	2 eggs, slightly beaten (at room temperature)
1 cup milk	3½ cups sifted all-purpose flour
⅓ cup sugar	1¾ cups yellow corn meal
1 teaspoon salt	1 tablespoon chili powder
1 teaspoon onion salt	¾ cup chopped ripe olives
¼ cup butter	
½ cup warm water (105° to 115°F.)	
2 packages active dry yeast	

1. In skillet, sauté bacon slices until crisp. Drain on paper towels, reserving ¼ cup drippings.

2. Crumble bacon; measure ¼ cup; set aside.

3. Heat milk just until bubbles form around edge of pan. Stir in sugar, salts, butter, and reserved bacon drippings. Let cool to lukewarm.

4. If possible, check temperature of warm water with thermometer. Sprinkle yeast over warm water in large, warm bowl. Stir to dissolve.

5. Stir lukewarm milk mixture, beaten eggs, flour, corn meal, and chili powder into yeast mixture. Beat vigorously with wooden spoon until well blended—about 2 minutes.

6. Cover with towel; let rise in warm place (85°F.), free from drafts, until double in bulk—about 1 hour.

7. Meanwhile, preheat oven to 375°F. Lightly grease a 2-quart casserole.

8. With wooden spoon, stir down batter. Beat in olives and bacon until well blended. Turn into prepared casserole.

9. Bake 35 to 40 minutes, or until nicely browned.

10. Remove from casserole to wire rack. Let cool completely, or serve slightly warm. Cut into wedges.

Makes 1 round loaf.

Toasted Hard Rolls

⅓ cup soft butter
2 tablespoons
    brown sugar

3 brown-and-serve club rolls,
    split lengthwise

1. Preheat oven to 400°F.
2. Mix butter and sugar well.
3. Spread cut sides of rolls with butter mixture.
4. Bake on cookie sheet 10 to 15 minutes, or until nicely browned.
Makes 6 servings.

Conchas

½ cup milk
½ cup sugar
¼ cup butter
1 teaspoon salt
½ cup warm water
    (105° to 115°F.)
1 package active dry
    yeast
2 eggs

3¾ cups sifted all-
    purpose flour

Topping
½ cup sugar
¼ cup butter
1 egg yolk
½ cup flour
1 teaspoon cinnamon

1. In small saucepan, heat milk until bubbles form around edge of pan; remove from heat.

2. Add ½ cup sugar, ¼ cup butter, and the salt, stirring until butter is melted. Let cool to lukewarm.

3. If possible, check temperature of warm water with thermometer. Sprinkle yeast over water in large bowl, stirring until dissolved. Add milk mixture.

4. Add 2 eggs and 2 cups flour; with electric mixer at medium speed, beat for 2 minutes. Add 1¾ cups flour; beat with wooden spoon until smooth and leaves side of bowl.

5. Turn dough onto lightly floured surface; knead until satiny and smooth. Add more flour, if needed, to keep dough from sticking.

6. Place in lightly greased bowl; turn to bring greased side up. Cover

with towel; let rise in warm place (85°F.), free from drafts, until double in bulk—about 1 hour.

7. Punch down dough; turn onto lightly floured surface. Knead 10 to 15 times. Shape into a roll about 12 inches long.

8. Cut roll crosswise into 12 pieces. Shape each piece into a ball. Place, smooth side up and 5 inches apart, on lightly greased cookie sheet. With palm of hand, flatten each ball into a 3-inch round.

9. Make topping: Cream sugar and butter until light and fluffy. Beat in egg yolk; blend in flour and cinnamon. Divide into 12 parts.

10. With palm of hand, flatten each part into a 2½-inch round, and place on a round of dough. Score topping with a sharp knife to look like a shell.

11. Cover with towel; let rise in warm place, free from drafts, until double in bulk—about 1 hour.

12. Preheat oven to 375°F.

13. Bake rolls 15 to 20 minutes, or until golden brown. Serve warm. Makes 12 rolls.

Mexican Churros

¼ cup butter, cut into small pieces	3 eggs
½ cup water	¼ teaspoon vanilla extract
⅛ teaspoon salt	Salad oil for deep-frying
1¼ cups sifted all-purpose flour	½ teaspoon cinnamon
	½ cup sugar

1. In medium saucepan, combine butter with ½ cup water. Stir over low heat until butter is melted. Bring just to boiling; add salt and remove from heat.

2. Add flour all at once; beat very hard with wooden spoon. Over low heat, beat until very smooth—about 2 minutes.

3. Remove from heat; let cool slightly. Beat in eggs, one at a time, beating well after each addition. Add vanilla. Continue beating until mixture has satinlike sheen.

4. Meanwhile, in deep skillet or deep-fat fryer, slowly heat salad oil (at least 1½ inches) to 380°F. on deep-frying thermometer.

5. Press the doughnut mixture through a large pastry bag with a large, fluted tip, ½ inch wide. With wet scissors, cut batter into 2-inch lengths as it drops into hot oil.

6. Deep-fry, a few at a time, 2 minutes on a side, or until golden brown.

7. Lift out with slotted spoon; drain well on paper towels.

8. Meanwhile, combine cinnamon and sugar in medium bowl.

9. Toss drained churros in sugar mixture to coat well. Serve warm. Makes about 24.

Buñuelos

2 cups unsifted all-purpose flour	6 tablespoons milk
2 tablespoons granulated sugar	2 tablespoons butter, melted
½ teaspoon salt	
2 eggs	Salad oil for deep-frying

1. In medium bowl, combine flour, granulated sugar, and salt. In small bowl, beat eggs; add milk and melted butter.

2. Add egg mixture to flour mixture; stir with fork until mixture holds together.

3. Turn dough onto lightly floured surface. Knead gently until smooth —3 to 5 minutes.

4. In electric skillet or heavy saucepan, slowly heat oil (1½ to 2 inches deep) to 375°F. on deep-frying thermometer.

5. Divide dough into 24 pieces. Shape each into a ball; roll out each, on lightly floured surface, to make a 5-inch round.

6. Gently drop rounds, a few at a time, into hot oil. Cook, turning with a slotted utensil, until they are lightly browned on both sides—about 2 to 3 minutes.

7. Drain on paper towels. Drizzle with cinnamon-sugar syrup while still warm.

Makes 2 dozen.

Cinnamon-Sugar Syrup

1½ cups sugar	2 tablespoons corn syrup
1 cup water	½ teaspoon cinnamon

1. In small saucepan, combine sugar, water, corn syrup, and cinnamon.

2. Boil, uncovered, 15 minutes, until slightly thickened, or to 220°F. on candy thermometer.

Makes 1½ cups.

Mocha Cake

½ cup milk	¼ teaspoon salt
1 cup sifted all-	3 eggs (⅔ cup)
purpose flour	1 cup sugar
1 teaspoon baking powder	1 teaspoon vanilla extract

1. In small saucepan, heat milk until bubbles form around edge of pan. Remove from heat; set aside.

2. Preheat oven to 350°F. Sift flour with baking powder and salt; set aside.

3. In small bowl of electric mixer, at high speed, beat eggs until thick and lemon-colored. Gradually add sugar, beating until mixture is smooth and well blended—about 5 minutes.

4. At low speed, blend in flour mixture just until smooth. Then add warm milk and the vanilla, beating just until combined.

5. Pour batter immediately into 2 ungreased 8-by-1½-inch layer-cake pans.

6. Bake 25 to 30 minutes, or until cake tester inserted in center comes out clean. Cool in pans on wire rack 10 minutes. Remove from pans; cool thoroughly on rack.

7. With a long, serrated knife, split each layer in half, to make 4 layers.

8. Put layers together with mocha butter cream (see below), using about ½ cup between each 2 layers. Frost top and side with remaining butter cream, swirling attractively. Pile chocolate curls on top of cake.

9. Refrigerate until serving time.

Makes 8 servings.

Mocha Butter Cream and Chocolate Curls

1 bar (9-ounce size)	2 cups confectioners' sugar
milk chocolate	⅓ cup strong coffee
½ cup butter	1 teaspoon vanilla extract
1 egg yolk	⅛ teaspoon salt

1. In top of double boiler, combine 6 ounces chocolate and the butter. (Set aside remaining chocolate.) Melt over hot, not boiling, water, stirring occasionally. Stir in egg yolk. Remove from hot water.

2. Blend in sugar, coffee, vanilla, and salt until smooth.

3. Place top of double boiler in pan of ice water. With electric mixer

at high speed, beat frosting until fluffy and of spreading consistency—about 5 minutes.

4. With vegetable parer, shave remaining chocolate into curls. Or, if desired, grate on a coarse grater.

Makes enough to fill and frost an 8-inch 4-layer cake.

Chocolate-Coconut Angel Cake

1 7- or 8-inch angel cake	1 can (3½-ounce size)
1 can (1-pound size)	flaked coconut
chocolate pudding	
1 pint frozen whipped	Chocolate shot (optional)
topping	

1. Split angel cake into three even layers. To make frosting, stir chocolate pudding and frozen whipped topping in medium bowl until they are smooth and well combined.

2. Spread ½ cup frosting on bottom layer of cake. Add middle layer, and spread with another ½ cup frosting. Top with last layer; spread remaining frosting over entire cake. Sprinkle generously with flaked coconut. Sprinkle top with chocolate shot. Place cake in refrigerator until dessert time.

Makes 6 to 8 servings.

Almond Torte

Pastry

1 package (11¼-ounce size)	1½ cups granulated sugar
pie-crust mix	Dash salt
2 tablespoons	2 teaspoons vanilla extract
granulated sugar	1 teaspoon almond extract
Ice water	3 egg whites
¼ cup firm butter	1 cup heavy cream,
	whipped

Almond-Cream Filling

2 envelopes unflavored	Confectioners' sugar
gelatin	⅓ cup ground peanut brittle or
4 cups milk	finely chopped toasted
3 egg yolks	almonds

1. Make pastry: In medium bowl, combine pie-crust mix and 2 tablespoons granulated sugar. Blend in ice water as package label directs. Shape pastry into a ball.

2. On lightly floured surface, roll out pastry to a 15-inch circle. Cut butter into small pieces; dot over pastry.

3. Fold pastry in thirds, one side overlapping the other; press edges together to seal. Fold again in thirds, from each end, and seal. Wrap in waxed paper. Refrigerate 30 minutes.

4. Meanwhile, make almond-cream filling: Sprinkle gelatin over ½ cup milk in top of double boiler, to soften. Add remaining milk. Place over direct heat, stirring, until tiny bubbles appear around edge of pan.

5. In medium bowl, beat egg yolks with ½ cup granulated sugar and the salt. Gradually stir in hot milk mixture. Return to top of double boiler.

6. Cook over simmering water, stirring constantly, 15 minutes. Remove from heat; stir in extracts. Strain into a large bowl. Refrigerate, covered and stirring occasionally, until mixture mounds slightly.

7. Meanwhile, shape pastry: Preheat oven to 425°F. Divide chilled pastry into quarters. On lightly floured surface, roll one quarter into an 8½-inch circle; using inverted 8-inch layer-cake pan as guide, cut into a perfect circle. Repeat with remaining quarters. Save trimmings.

8. Place on cookie sheets. With fork, prick each round well; sprinkle each with 1 teaspoon granulated sugar. Bake 8 minutes, or until golden.

9. Reroll trimmings to a 10-by-5-inch rectangle; sprinkle with 1 teaspoon granulated sugar. Fold in half lengthwise; roll again into a 10-by-5-inch rectangle. With 2-inch cookie cutter, cut pastry into rounds; cut out centers with 1-inch cutter, to make rings. Reroll and cut trimmings, to make as many rings as possible. Place on cookie sheet. Bake 5 minutes, or until golden.

10. With electric mixer at high speed, beat egg whites until soft peaks form when beater is slowly raised. Gradually beat in remaining ½ cup granulated sugar. Continue beating until stiff peaks form.

11. Fold egg whites and whipped cream into chilled gelatin mixture, blending well.

12. In an 8-inch springform pan, layer pastry circles and filling, beginning with pastry and ending with filling.

13. Refrigerate until firm—at least 4 hours.

14. To serve: Sprinkle pastry rings generously with confectioners' sugar. Place on top of torte. Remove side from springform, and sprinkle side of torte with peanut brittle.

Makes 12 servings.

Cinnamon Teacakes

1 cup butter	1 teaspoon cinnamon
1½ cups confectioners' sugar	¼ teaspoon salt
2¼ cups sifted all-purpose flour	1 teaspoon vanilla extract

1. In large bowl of electric mixer, cream butter until light and fluffy. Then, at low speed, blend in ½ cup sugar, flour, ½ teaspoon cinnamon, salt, and vanilla extract (dough will be rather stiff).

2. Chill in refrigerator 30 minutes, or until stiff enough to handle easily.

3. Preheat oven to 400°F. Roll dough between fingers into 1-inch balls. Place the balls 2 inches apart on lightly greased cookie sheets; bake 9 to 10 minutes, or until a delicate golden brown color.

4. On piece of waxed paper, combine remaining sugar and cinnamon. Roll hot teacakes in this mixture; place on wire racks to cool.

Makes about 3½ dozen.

Mexican Cookie Kisses

1 cup sifted all-purpose flour	⅛ teaspoon nutmeg
⅛ teaspoon baking soda	1 teaspoon cinnamon
	½ cup soft butter
	1 cup sugar

1. Preheat oven to 400°F. Sift flour with baking soda, nutmeg, and cinnamon; set aside.

2. In large bowl of electric mixer, at medium speed, beat butter with sugar until very light and fluffy.

3. At low speed, beat in flour mixture just until well combined.

4. On lightly floured surface, roll dough ¼ inch thick. Using 2-inch star- and heart-shaped cookie cutters, cut out dough. Reroll, and cut out leftover dough.

5. Place on ungreased cookie sheets, 1½ inches apart; bake 8 to 10 minutes.

6. Remove from oven; let stand on cookie sheets about 2 minutes. Remove to wire rack.

Makes about 4 dozen.

Almond Cookies

1⅔ cups whole blanched almonds	Dash salt
2 egg whites	⅔ cup sugar

1. Preheat oven to 350°F. Spread 1⅓ cups almonds in a shallow baking pan; bake 10 minutes, or until toasted and nicely browned.

2. Finely grind almonds, using food chopper or blender. Set aside.

3. In medium bowl, with portable electric mixer, beat egg whites with salt until foamy.

4. Add sugar, 2 tablespoons at a time, beating well after each addition. Continue beating until stiff peaks form when beater is raised.

5. Fold in ground nuts—mixture should be thick and hold its shape.

6. Drop by heaping teaspoonfuls, 1 inch apart, on well-greased cookie sheet. Top each with one of the remaining whole almonds.

7. Bake 7 to 10 minutes, or just until lightly browned. Remove from cookie sheets at once; cool on wire rack. Store in airtight container.

Makes about 3 dozen.

Mexican Cinnamon Cookies

1 cup butter, softened	1 teaspoon vanilla extract
½ cup confectioners' sugar	¼ teaspoon salt
2¼ cups sifted all-purpose flour	½ cup granulated sugar, or ¾ cup confectioners' sugar
1 teaspoon cinnamon	½ teaspoon cinnamon

1. In large bowl, with electric mixer at high speed, beat butter until light and fluffy.

2. At low speed, beat in ½ cup confectioners' sugar, the flour, 1 teaspoon cinnamon, the vanilla, and salt just until combined—dough will be rather stiff.

3. Shape into a ball; wrap in waxed paper. Refrigerate 30 minutes.

4. Preheat oven to 400°F.

5. To make ball cookies, roll dough into ¾-inch balls. To make flat cookies, roll into 1-inch balls; flatten with fingers to about ¼-inch thickness. Place 1½ inches apart on ungreased cookie sheets.

6. Bake 10 minutes, or until a delicate golden brown.

7. Combine sugar and cinnamon. Roll hot cookies in this mixture. Place on wire rack to cool; sprinkle with any remaining cinnamon-sugar.

Makes about 5 dozen ball cookies or 3 dozen flat cookies.

Desserts &
Sweet Drinks

Mexicans have a penchant for sweets and elaborate desserts, a fondness that makes great sense when you consider that they were the people who first revealed the delights of both chocolate and vanilla to the rest of the world. Within hours after arriving at Montezuma's court, the Spanish conquistadors were permitted to speak to the king at his breakfast table. There they found him drinking a dark liquid which one of the Spaniards later tasted and found to be "of a very exciting nature." It was chocolate that Montezuma was drinking, served to him chilled with bits of snow from the high mountains nearby and flavored with what the Spanish later came to call vanilla. Chocolate drinks, hot or cold and flavored with vanilla, are drunk throughout Mexico today by adults and children alike, and chocolate desserts, such as chocolate balls and chocolate mousse, are immensely popular.

Other Mexican desserts display the country's connection with Spain. Frequently served are flan, or caramel custard, and royal eggs, desserts that are as Spanish as they are Mexican. But whatever its origins, dessert to a Mexican is an integral part of a good dinner; it displays the cook's final concern with delighting her guests.

Caramel Custard

1¼ cups sugar
4 eggs
1 can (14½-ounce size)
   evaporated milk,
   undiluted

1½ cups water
1 teaspoon vanilla extract
Whole blanched almonds
Whipped cream

1. Preheat oven to 350°F.

2. Spread ½ cup sugar evenly over bottom of an 8-inch round baking dish. Heat in oven 30 to 35 minutes, or until sugar is melted to a golden brown syrup.

3. Remove from oven; let cool 10 minutes, or until hardened.

4. Meanwhile, in medium bowl, with rotary beater, beat eggs well. Add ¾ cup sugar, the evaporated milk, the water, and the vanilla; stir until sugar is dissolved.

5. Pour into prepared baking dish. Place in shallow pan; pour hot water to 1-inch level around dish.

6. Bake 1 hour, or until silver knife inserted in center of custard comes out clean. Cool; then refrigerate until well chilled.

7. To serve: Run small spatula around edge of dish to loosen. Invert onto shallow serving dish. Decorate with almonds and whipped cream.

Makes 6 servings.

Brandied Caramel Flan

¾ cup sugar

Custard
2 cups milk
2 cups light cream
6 eggs
½ cup sugar

½ teaspoon salt
2 teaspoons vanilla extract
⅓ cup brandy
Boiling water

1 tablespoon brandy

1. Place ¾ cup sugar in a large, heavy skillet. Cook, over medium heat, until sugar melts and forms a light brown syrup; stir to blend.

2. Immediately pour syrup into a heated 8¼-inch round, shallow baking dish; holding dish with pot holders, quickly rotate, to cover bottom and side completely. Set aside.

3. Preheat oven to 325°F.

4. Make custard: In medium saucepan, heat milk and cream just until bubbles form around edge of pan.

5. In large bowl, with rotary beater, beat eggs slightly. Add sugar, salt, and vanilla. Gradually stir in hot milk mixture and ⅓ cup brandy. Pour into prepared dish.

6. Set dish in shallow pan; pour boiling water to ½-inch level around dish.

7. Bake 35 to 40 minutes, or until silver knife inserted in center comes out clean. Let custard cool; refrigerate 4 hours or overnight.

8. To serve: Run small spatula around edge of dish, to loosen. Invert on shallow serving dish; shake gently to release. The caramel acts as sauce. Warm 1 tablespoon brandy slightly; ignite, and quickly pour over flan.

Makes 8 servings.

Cold Caramel Soufflé

12 egg whites
(1⅔ cups)

2 packages (1-pound size)
superfine granulated sugar

1. In large bowl of electric mixer, let egg whites warm to room temperature—about 1 hour.

2. Meanwhile, place 1½ cups sugar in a heavy, medium skillet. To caramelize, cook over high heat, stirring, until sugar is completely melted and begins to boil—syrup should be a medium brown.

3. Hold a 3-quart oven-glassware casserole with pot holder, and pour in hot syrup all at once. Tilt and rotate casserole until bottom and sides are thoroughly coated. Set on wire rack, and let cool.

4. Beat egg whites, at high speed, until very stiff—about 8 minutes.

5. While continuing to beat, gradually pour in 1 package sugar, in a continuous stream—takes about 3 minutes. Scrape side of bowl with rubber scraper. Beat 15 minutes.

6. Meanwhile (about 5 minutes before beating time is up), place ¾ cup sugar in heavy, medium skillet, and caramelize as in step 2. Remove from heat, and immediately place skillet in pan of cold water for 20 to 30 seconds, or until syrup is thick; stir constantly.

7. With beater at medium speed, gradually pour syrup into beaten egg-white mixture. Scrape side of bowl with rubber scraper. Return to high speed, and beat 12 minutes longer.

8. Preheat oven to 250°F.

9. Turn egg-white mixture into prepared casserole, spreading evenly. Set in large baking pan; pour boiling water to 1-inch depth around casserole.

10. Bake 1 hour, or until meringue seems firm when gently shaken and rises about 1 inch above casserole.

11. Meanwhile, make English custard sauce (see below).

12. Remove casserole from water; place on wire rack to cool. Refrigerate until very well chilled—6 hours or overnight.

13. To unmold: Run a small spatula around edge of meringue, to loosen. Hold casserole in pan of very hot water at least 1 minute. Invert onto serving dish.

14. Pour some of the sauce over meringue, and pass the rest.

Makes 16 servings.

English Custard Sauce

¾ cup sugar	12 egg yolks
2 tablespoons cornstarch	1 tablespoon vanilla extract
1 quart milk	1 cup heavy cream
4 tablespoons butter	

1. In medium saucepan, combine sugar and cornstarch. Gradually add milk; stir until smooth. Add butter.

2. Cook over medium heat, stirring constantly, until mixture is thickened and comes to boil. Boil 1 minute. Remove from heat.

3. In medium bowl, slightly beat egg yolks. Gradually add a little hot mixture, beating well.

4. Stir into rest of hot mixture; cook over medium heat, stirring constantly, just until mixture boils. Remove from heat; stir in vanilla.

5. Strain custard immediately into bowl. Refrigerate, covered, until cool. Stir in heavy cream. Return to refrigerator until well chilled.

Makes about 6 cups.

Royal Eggs

12 egg yolks	1 3-inch cinnamon stick,
Boiling water	broken into small pieces
1¾ cups sugar	⅓ cup sherry
2½ cups water	

1. Preheat oven to 350°F. Butter bottom and sides of a 9-by-5-by-3-inch loaf pan.

2. In small bowl of electric mixer, at medium speed, beat egg yolks until very thick and lemon-colored—about 7 minutes. Pour into prepared pan.

3. Place loaf pan in shallow baking pan. Pour boiling water to 1-inch depth around loaf pan.

4. Bake 20 minutes, or until cake tester inserted in center comes out clean. Remove to wire rack, and let cool in pan.

5. In medium saucepan, combine sugar with water and cinnamon stick. Bring to boiling, stirring until sugar is dissolved. Boil 5 minutes.

6. Cut cooled egg mixture into 12 cubes. Put a piece of cinnamon stick from syrup in each. Turn cubes into syrup; simmer gently, uncovered, 10 minutes. Remove from heat; stir in sherry.

7. Cool; refrigerate, covered, for at least 24 hours.

Makes 12 servings.

Chocolate Balls

1 can (14-ounce size) sweetened condensed milk	3 jars (1-ounce size) chocolate shot
4 ounces sweet cooking chocolate	

1. In medium saucepan, combine condensed milk and chocolate. Cook over medium heat, stirring constantly, until mixture is boiling.

2. Reduce heat, and cook, stirring constantly, 5 minutes, or until the mixture mounds and leaves side of the pan.

3. Remove from heat; let cool until easy to handle—about 45 minutes.

4. Using hands, roll mixture into balls about ¾ inch in diameter. Roll in chocolate shot.

Makes about 3 dozen.

Note: These candies will keep about 10 days if refrigerated, in a single layer, in a tightly covered container.

Chocolate Mousse

2½ cups sweet butter	1½ cups finely chopped walnuts or pecans
2 cups superfine granulated sugar	6 egg whites
6 egg yolks	1 cup heavy cream, whipped
16 ounces sweet cooking chocolate, melted	
¼ cup cognac	Fresh strawberries

1. In large bowl of electric mixer, at high speed, beat butter and sugar until very light and fluffy—20 minutes.

2. Add egg yolks, one at a time, beating well after each addition. Gradually beat in chocolate; continue beating 3 minutes longer.

3. Add cognac; beat 3 minutes. Mix in nuts.

4. In another large bowl, beat egg whites until soft peaks form when beater is slowly raised. Fold in chocolate mixture until thoroughly mixed. Pour into 2-quart ring mold.

5. Refrigerate until well chilled—at least 3 hours.

6. To serve: Unmold onto serving plate. Fill center with whipped cream. Garnish with fresh strawberries.

Makes 20 servings.

Chocolate-Cinnamon Ice Cream

1 vanilla bean	¼ teaspoon salt
4 cups light cream	6 ounces semisweet
4 egg yolks	chocolate
1 cup sugar	2 tablespoons cinnamon
1 tablespoon cornstarch	1½ cups heavy cream

1. Split vanilla bean; with tip of knife, scrape seeds into light cream in a medium saucepan. Heat until bubbles appear around edge of pan.

2. In medium bowl, beat egg yolks with sugar, cornstarch, and salt until well combined. Gradually stir in hot cream. Return to saucepan; cook over medium heat, stirring constantly, until mixture is thickened and just comes to boiling.

3. Add chocolate and cinnamon. Remove from heat; stir until chocolate is melted. Set aside until cool.

4. Stir in heavy cream.

5. To freeze in 1-quart crank-type freezer (see *Note*): Pour half of chocolate mixture into freezer container; insert dasher, and close container tightly. Pack freezer with ice and coarse salt in 4-to-1 proportion. Crank for 15 minutes, or until dasher is difficult to turn.

6. Serve immediately or spoon into freezer containers and place in freezer. Freeze other half. Serve with prepared bittersweet-chocolate sauce.

Makes about 2 quarts.

Note: If using an electric freezer, follow manufacturer's directions.

Chocolate-Meringue Pudding

16 to 18 ounces chocolate pudding	2 egg whites
½ teaspoon cinnamon	¼ cup sugar
	1 tablespoon sliced almonds

1. Turn chocolate pudding into 1-quart shallow baking dish. Stir in cinnamon, to mix well.

2. In medium bowl, with electric mixer, beat egg whites until soft peaks form. Gradually beat in sugar until stiff peaks form.

3. Spread meringue over chocolate pudding to edge of dish, making swirls over top. Sprinkle with almonds. Bake, at 400°F., 5 to 6 minutes, or until golden.

4. Remove to wire rack; cool 10 minutes. Serve slightly warm.

Makes 5 to 6 servings.

Pink and Yellow Coconut Apples

1½ cups granulated sugar	Red food coloring
½ cup milk	Yellow food coloring
¼ teaspoon cream of tartar	Superfine granulated sugar
1 package (7-ounce size) finely grated coconut	Raisins

1. In medium saucepan, combine granulated sugar, milk, and cream of tartar. Cook over high heat, stirring, until sugar is dissolved and mixture comes to boiling. Boil to 225°F. on candy thermometer.

2. Remove from heat. Stir in coconut.

3. Divide in half into 2 small bowls. With food color, tint one half pink, the other pale yellow. Cool at room temperature—about 2 hours.

4. Using hands, roll mixture into balls about 1½ inches in diameter. Roll in superfine sugar. Press a raisin in top of each.

Makes about 1½ dozen.

Note: These are at their best if made no more than two days ahead.

Cinnamon Oranges

3 oranges	¼ teaspoon cinnamon
¼ cup sugar	

1. Peel oranges; slice crosswise, ¼ inch thick. Arrange in shallow dish.

2. Combine sugar and cinnamon. Toss oranges with sugar mixture, to coat well. Refrigerate until well chilled—at least 1 hour.

Makes 6 servings.

Fruit Platter

1 pink grapefruit	**Dressing**
½ cantaloupe	¾ cup honey
1 2-pound watermelon	½ cup lemon juice

1. Peel grapefruit; remove any white membrane. Then section the grapefruit.

2. Peel cantaloupe; cut into thin slices with sharp knife.

3. Cut watermelon into 1-inch chunks, removing as many seeds as possible.

4. Arrange fruit on salad platter. Refrigerate, covered with plastic wrap, until well chilled—about 2 hours.

5. Also, make dressing: In small bowl, with rotary beater, beat honey with lemon juice. Refrigerate along with fruit until well chilled.

6. Serve fruit with dressing.

Makes 4 to 6 servings.

Mexican Hot Chocolate

¼ cup unsweetened cocoa	Dash salt
	1 quart milk
¼ cup sugar	¼ cup light cream
¾ teaspoon cinnamon	¾ teaspoon vanilla extract

1. In small bowl, combine cocoa, sugar, cinnamon, and salt; mix well.

2. In medium saucepan, heat 1 cup milk until bubbling. Stir in cocoa mixture; beat with wire whisk or rotary beater until smooth.

3. Over low heat, bring to boiling, stirring. Gradually stir in rest of milk; return to boiling.

4. Stir in cream and vanilla; heat gently.

5. Before serving, beat with rotary beater until frothy.

Makes 6 servings.

Mexican Coffee

4 cups water	2 3-inch cinnamon sticks
⅓ cup dark-brown sugar, firmly packed	½ cup ground coffee

1. In medium saucepan, combine water, sugar, and cinnamon. Bring to boiling, stirring until sugar is dissolved; reduce heat, and simmer, covered, about 5 minutes.

2. Stir in coffee; simmer, uncovered, 2 minutes. Remove from heat. Stir; cover, and let stand in warm place until coffee grounds settle—about 5 minutes. Carefully pour into heated coffeepot or cups.

Makes 4 servings.

Index